The Ultimate Birthday Book

The Ultimate Birthday Book

TRACEY TURNER

PICCADILLY PRESS • LONDON

*For Toby James Battersby, whose birthday is on the 28th February.
And for Jane Burnard, who is full of bright ideas, including this one.*

First published in Great Britain in 2006
by Piccadilly Press Ltd,
5 Castle Road, London NW1 8PR
www.piccadillypress.co.uk

Text copyright © Tracey Turner, 2006
Illustrations copyright © Sue Hellard, 2006

All rights reserved. No part of this publication may be reproduced, stored
in a retrieval system, or transmitted in any form or by any means,
electronic, mechanical, photocopying, recording or otherwise, without the
prior permission of the copyright owner.

The right of Tracey Turner to be identified as Author of this work has
been asserted by her in accordance with the Copyright, Designs and
Patents Act 1988

A catalogue record for this book is available from the British Library

ISBN: 1 85340 829 8 (trade paperback)
ISBN-13: 9 781853 408298

1 3 5 7 9 10 8 6 4 2

Printed and bound in Great Britain by Bookmarque Ltd
Typeset by M Rules, London
Set in 11/14 Gill Sans Book and Melanie
Cover design by Simon Davis
Illustrations by Sue Hellard

Papers used by Piccadilly Press are produced from forests grown and managed as a
renewable resource, and which conform to the requirements of recognised
forestry accreditation schemes.

Contents

Introduction **7**

1. Perfect Parties **9**

2. Birthday Treats, Sleepovers and Surprises **49**

3. Perfect Presents, Cards and Cakes **71**

4. Birthdays Through the Year **99**

Introduction

Wherever they live and however old they are, almost everyone celebrates the day they were born. This book tells you everything you need to know (plus a bit extra) for making birthdays special. There are ideas for:

- birthday party themes (including an indoor beach party)
- birthday presents (including how to make a birthday cracker)
- birthday party games (old, new and very silly indeed)
- birthday pampering (for yourself and your friends)
- how to spring a surprise birthday celebration

. . . and Chapter 4 even has information on star signs, birthstones and birth flowers for every month, as well as famous events and celebrity birthdays for each day.

Read on and find out how to celebrate in style . . .

"Birthdays are good for you.
The more you have, the longer you live."
— Anonymous

Chapter 1
PERFECT PARTIES

You can't have a successful birthday party if you just phone a few of your mates on the day, buy a couple of bottles of cheap coke and hope for the best. There's no getting away from it: parties need planning and effort. But the good news is that this can be as much fun as the party.

Planning Makes Perfect

If you want to avoid a panic, make sure you allow plenty of time to organise everything. Draw up a list a few weeks in advance so that you don't suddenly remember something on the day of the party – like inviting people! – and have to be sedated. The ideal scenario is to be able to have fun with a couple of mates while you're setting up the party, then have an hour or so free to lounge about admiring your efforts.

Things to do in the weeks leading up to the party:
* make a guest list and send out your invitations
* make some party CDs or sort out playlists on your MP3 player
* decide what food and drink you're going to make and try out some recipes if you want to
* decide what you're going to wear and buy anything you need/can afford

Things to do a day or two before the party:
✷ go shopping for food and drink
✷ make any food that will keep until the party and put it in the fridge
✷ put up decorations (unless they're going to get in the way)
✷ sort out your music so that you have at your fingertips all the CDs you want to play
✷ make sure you know where everything is

Things to do on the day of the party:
✷ make any food you couldn't make in advance
✷ make your venue safe and secure
✷ put the finishing touches to your decorations
✷ set out food and drink
✷ get dressed, hang out with your mates, and relax

Birthday Party Rules
DO...
- ✓ let people know what time the party will begin and end. You don't want people to arrive in dribs and drabs, or to have to chase them out with a broom in the early hours of the morning.
- ✓ send out written invitations – don't just text message or email (see page 12.)
- ✓ wear an outfit that makes you feel special, but not something that's going to make you feel uncomfortable (either mentally or physically!) (see page 30).
- ✓ make sure there's plenty of music and put someone in charge of it (one of your friends is bound to be a born DJ).
- ✓ have a few games ready to play (though these should not be compulsory: no one should be forced to play Twister!) (see page 40).
- ✓ provide plenty of delicious food and drink – don't limit this to a trough full of crisps and some flat lemonade (see page 31).

Planning Makes Perfect

- ✓ let the neighbours know about the party.
- ✓ decide in advance on any areas that are off limits and lock doors if possible.
- ✓ remove or protect anything that's breakable or that could get ruined (e.g. take up rugs, and perhaps cover your mum's favourite cream-coloured sofa with a throw).
- ✓ make sure everyone can get home OK – don't let anyone stumble off into the night on their own.
- ✓ get hold of an adult *straight away* if there's any trouble (e.g. gatecrashers).
- ✓ remember to have fun!

DON'T...

- ✗ be tempted to invite twice as many people as will fit into the available space.
- ✗ lock your little brothers and sisters in a cupboard. (But do take measures to make sure they behave themselves – see page 47.)
- ✗ lock your parents in a cupboard. (But see advice for coping with them on page 45.)
- ✗ provide alcohol, or let anyone bring any. (If you break this rule, remember that staggering about drooling is *so* not a sophisticated look.)
- ✗ allow smoking. It'll take for ever to get rid of the pong.
- ✗ make anyone feel bad if they want to leave early.

Glamorous Guest List

Whether you're having your party in your home or at a special venue, work out how many people you can comfortably fit into the available space and *don't* be tempted to invite twice that number on the basis that half of them probably won't be able to come. If the party's in your home, keep the number to under thirty (even if you live in a mansion). The idea is to have fun with your friends, not crush them to death.

Of course, you'll want to invite all your close friends, and you might want to invite some people you don't know so well but would like to get to know better. This might possibly be someone you fancy . . . but *beware* of this becoming an obsession – if things work out the way you want, you'll spend the evening mooning and snogging and ignoring your friends; if things go badly and the object of your affections starts chatting up your best mate, you could find it impossible not to burst into tears and send everyone home.

Interesting Invitations

Send or give out written invitations – don't just text or email people. This will let them know that the party is something you're putting time and effort into, and they won't feel tempted to forward the email or text to five hundred of their friends.

Your invitation sets the tone for the whole party, and you don't want your guests to expect a dingy living room, a couple of cans of coke and a few people sitting around looking bored. So put some effort into your invites. You can buy invitations, of course, but you can make much classier ones yourself for half the money (but a bit more time and effort). If you don't like craft projects, a halfway measure is to buy some very plain invites and jazz them up a bit yourself: you could add a little picture of your own on each one (even if it's just a squiggle) to make them personal, use gold or silver pen to make them look a bit special, and you could even dot some glitter about. But if you do have the time and the inclination to make your own invitations from scratch, here are one or two ideas.

Simple but Stylish

It's often best to keep things simple. Cut out a postcard-sized rectangle of fairly stiff card, any colour you like. (You could also use plain postcards and spray-paint the plain side, or buy plain cards to decorate from craft shops and stationers.) Add a list of details along the lines of:

Who:
Mo is invited to . . .

What:
A party!

When:
7.30 –11.00 p.m. on 3 July

Where:
14 Grove Road

Why:
To celebrate Jess's birthday

Then add some spirals or stars, or just dots of glitter-coloured glue. Use a metallic pen or a colour that contrasts well with the colour of your card.

Shapes

With a little bit more effort you could cut out shapes for your invitations: stars, circles, witches' hats, sunglasses (they take some effort but look cool), flowers, hearts – anything you fancy, or that ties in with the theme of your party (if you have one). Or, if you can, scan a photo of your favourite celeb (just their face looks good), copy it onto paper or card, and use cut-outs of it as your invites. Do try to keep the shapes regular – use something to draw around before you cut them out.

Paper Planes

Write your invitations on pieces of coloured A4 paper. Then make them into paper planes and aim them at your guests.

Balloon Invitations

Blow up a balloon and hold the end closed (get someone to do this for you, or secure it with a big paperclip). Write your invitation on the blown-up balloon with a marker pen. Then deflate the balloon and put it in an envelope – write *Blow Up The Balloon* on the back of the envelope.

Parchment Scrolls

Try these if you want to be a bit posh. Use fairly thick pieces of white paper, rub them with a used teabag on both sides and leave them to dry completely. They should now look like ye olde parchment. Write your invitation on each one, and you could add a map of how to get to the party (to look like a treasure map with X marking the spot). Roll them up and tie them with a piece of ribbon.

If in doubt about your invitations, less is usually more!

Party Themes

Chinese New Year Party

The Chinese New Year can occur any time between the middle of January and the middle of February – just when everyone needs a bit of cheering up – and it makes a great theme for a winter birthday party. Chinese New Year celebrations last for fifteen days, but sadly you'll have to condense your party into just a few hours.

生日快乐

Birthday Sharing

The seventh day of the Chinese New Year used to be a special time to celebrate birthdays – everybody's birthday. Individual birth dates were not considered to be as important as this date, and everyone added a year to their age on that day, instead of on their real birthday.

Invitations:
Make your invitations from red card and find a simple Chinese image as decoration – you could draw a Chinese character in black or gold pen. Don't forget to put your fancy dress instructions on the card where they can't be ignored!

What to wear:
Ask everyone to come as their Chinese horoscope animal (see page 16). Your friends will probably be about the same age and your Chinese horoscope depends on the year you were born, not the date, so the party is likely to be dominated by a couple of animals – although this might be difficult to tell from appearances! Give out a prize for the best two or three most common animals (e.g. the best rooster and the best dog) and add a special extra prize for artistic interpretation.

Decorations:
- Blossom is a traditional decoration for the Chinese New Year – go out and collect some fallen twigs and small branches, and glue on small pieces of scrunched-up pink tissue paper. Put them in vases as decoration.
- Red is a lucky colour in China. Hang wide pieces of red cloth or crêpe paper on the walls (make them at least 30 cm wide and at least 1 m long). Copy the Chinese script for 'Happy Birthday' on them (see opposite page) in thick black marker or poster paint.

* Bowls of tangerines and oranges are a traditional Chinese New Year decoration. (If you're visiting friends or relatives at Chinese New Year, you're supposed to bring some tangerines or oranges with you – preferably ones with the leaves still on them – for good luck.)
* Buy some Chinese lanterns and put tea-lights in them, and make your own paper lanterns (but don't be tempted to put candles in those unless you want to invite the fire brigade to your party).
* Find out which animal represents the New Year (see below) and put up a picture of the animal with a label.

Check Out Your Chinese Horoscope

Your Chinese horoscope depends on the year you were born. So if you were born in 1994 you're a dog, 1992 you're a monkey. Find out which animals you and your friends and family are:

Rat years: 1960, 1972, 1984, 1996, 2008
Ox years: 1961, 1973, 1985, 1997, 2009
Tiger years: 1962, 1974, 1986, 1998, 2010
Rabbit years: 1963, 1975, 1987, 1999
Dragon years: 1964, 1976, 1988, 2000
Snake years: 1965, 1977, 1989, 2001
Horse years: 1966, 1978, 1990, 2002
Sheep years: 1967, 1979, 1991, 2003
Monkey years: 1968, 1980, 1992, 2004
Rooster years: 1969, 1981, 1993, 2005
Dog years: 1970, 1982, 1994, 2006
Pig years: 1971, 1983, 1995, 2007

Oscars Party

The Academy Awards ceremony usually happens in spring, so if you have a spring birthday, what better way to celebrate than with an Oscars party?

> "Spring is nature's way of saying, 'Let's party!'"
> – Robin Williams

Invitations:

These should be extra posh – it's a prestigious event and your mates should think themselves very lucky to receive an invitation. Try plain white with gold-leaf lettering (or metallic gold pen if you've temporarily run out of gold-leaf) and use your calligraphy skills (or use a computer's – much easier). Don't forget to put all the relevant information on the invites – what time and where (22A, High Street, Hollywood), how people should dress, any highlights (e.g. an award ceremony), etc.

What to wear:

Designer dresses and dinner jackets, obviously. (Or as close as people can get – you don't really have to break the bank.)

Decorations:

A red carpet from the garden gate to your front door, or from the front door to the main party room, sets the tone nicely. It doesn't have to be a real carpet: you could use any red material, but make sure it's not your mum's new curtains. You might find you can buy a length of red material very cheaply if there's a local market. Take a photo of each glamorous guest as they sashay down the red carpet (it may be the closest they'll ever come to the paparazzi). Use understated decorations, perhaps in just one colour – a few well-placed balloons, perhaps some flower arrangements, and a cardboard cut-out (or several) of an Academy Award. Draw your award on a piece of cardboard (or get an artistic friend to do it for you), cut it out and spray it with gold paint – the bigger the better if it's going to form your centrepiece. Then you'll need a few smaller ones to give out in your awards ceremony (see below).

The Academy Awards ceremony:

Tell everyone in advance that there will be awards in various categories. Make up your own, but here are a few ideas . . .

* Best Actress (for a friend who's a drama queen, or who's managed to fool a teacher with an Oscar-winning performance, or who's good at drama)
* Best Actor (see above)
* Best Newcomer (for someone who's new to the area, perhaps)
* Best Costume Designer (for your best-dressed mate)
* Best Make-up (for your perfectly mascara-ed pal)
* Best Screenplay (for someone good at writing – perhaps they helped write the school play)
* Best Director (for someone who's a bit of a bossy-boots – in the nicest possible way, of course)
* Best Art Direction (this could be for the person who drew your Oscars for you)

Everyone should prepare an acceptance speech beforehand (thanking everyone, including the cat), and should practise weeping copiously. A small prize as well as the cardboard Oscar is in order – perhaps a box of chocs or a bunch of flowers. You could also have a film- or Oscars-related quiz, including plenty of fun film-star gossip. At the end, everyone swaps their answers and marks someone else's. The winner gets another prize.

# Retro Party

Have you ever wondered what it was like for your mum and dad when they were teenagers? Now's your chance to find out. Theme your party around the 1970s or 1980s (depending on how ancient your parents are, or which decade appeals to you more). Apart from having hysterics at your mates dressed in sequinned boob-tubes, it's a chance to quiz your parents on their teenage years, and to involve them in your party – which will make them worry about it less. Ask your parents about slang words, fashion and music (you could borrow some for the party, if they still have it), and do your own research, to give your party that authentic feel.

Invitations:

Use your computer skills for your invitations: choose a 70s- or 80s-style typeface and use an iconic image from the decade of your choice (the Bay City Rollers or Duran Duran, perhaps). It's a good idea to put some of your research into the envelope with the invitation – perhaps a list of slang words (with translations), a list of songs they might like to get to know before the party, and hilarious images of 70s or 80s fashion victims.

What to wear:

Have a good trawl through your research to find a look you think will suit you (you probably don't want to spend your birthday looking completely ridiculous). It might be that your parents can help you out here. Otherwise, charity shops are a good place to find authentic clothing cheaply.

Music:

You'll need to make sure that you and your friends don't totally hate the music beforehand, since an 80s party without 80s music seems a bit pointless. Retro CDs are easy to find and usually pretty cheap.

Beach Party

Beaches are great places for parties, but not many of us live near enough to a beach or have a birthday at the right time of year. Never mind – why not have a beach party anyway, even if it's raining? Simply bring the beach to your living room.

> "It is one of the blessings of old friends that you can afford to be stupid with them."
> – Ralph Waldo Emerson

What to wear:

Ask people to dress for the beach. This could mean lots of different things: surfing gear, a wetsuit, a bikini, a swimming costume or trunks, a large sunhat, T-shirt and shorts. But sunglasses are essential.

Decorations:

Raid the loft and look for anything with a vaguely beach or nautical theme. Decorate the party room with surfboards, beach balls, parasols, snorkels, rowing boats, fishing nets, a three-metre Great White replica . . .

Food:

Give out ice creams in cones, and get your little brother to wander about with a tray of cold drinks shouting "Cocacola! Limonada!" for that Euro-beach effect. If you can have your party on a real beach, or at least outside, a barbecue will give the best beach-party food. As well as the usual sausages and burgers, grill skewers of vegetables and fruit – halved mushrooms, chunks of red, green or yellow pepper, slices of onion and pineapple, whole baby sweetcorn – brushed with a little olive oil.

Hawaiian Luau

As a variation on the beach-party theme, why not have a Hawaiian *luau*? These are big, traditional Hawaiian parties, usually held on a beach. Each guest should be greeted in traditional Hawaiian style with a *lei* – a garland of flowers (the homemade paper flowers on page 29 are perfect for this if you string them together, or you could just stick one of the flowers in each guest's hair). You could even look up what the Hawaiian version of each guest's name is on the Internet!

What to wear:

Grass skirts, shirts and shorts in Hawaiian patterns, or anything summery in bright colours.

Decorations:

Decorate the room with plenty of fruit and flowers (either real or paper ones coloured bright yellow, orange and red). Make sure you include a couple of pineapples – these are very Hawaiian. Have a big bowl of fruit punch as the centrepiece.

Food:

The main traditional Hawaiian dish at a *luau* is a Kahlua pig roasted in an underground oven called an *imu*. You might not fancy slaughtering a pig and digging up the garden, but be sure to provide plenty of party food and include lots of exotic fruit and a fruit punch. You might want to try the easy Hawaiian dessert dish on the next page.

Haupia

WHAT YOU NEED:
1 can of coconut milk
5 tbsp sugar
5 tbsp cornflour
200 ml water
Shallow flapjack tin about 20 cm square

WHAT YOU DO:
- Pour the coconut milk into a saucepan.
- Mix the sugar and cornflour together, and add them to the pan with the water. On a low heat, stir the mixture continually, until it starts to thicken.
- Keep stirring until the mixture has completely thickened, and then pour it into the flapjack tin.
- Leave the mixture to cool, and then chill it in the fridge for a few hours until it's firm.
- Cut it into 5 cm squares and impress your guests with a delicious Hawaiian snack.

Garden Party

If you're lucky enough to have a decent-sized garden, why not swan about pretending to be royalty at your birthday garden party? If it rains you'll have to bring the party inside, of course, but you can still eat cucumber sandwiches and pretend to be aristocratic. To be really authentic you'll need to play croquet on the lawn.

What to wear:

Ask female guests to wear tiaras (it doesn't matter if they're made of cardboard, with glitter and sequins stuck on). The boys should wear straw boaters (these are hats, in case you're wondering), or bow ties.

Food:
Sip iced tea and eat cucumber sandwiches with the crusts cut off, like what posh people do.

> Double Birthdays
> Some VIPs, such as Queen Elizabeth II, have two birthdays – one on their real birthday and another on a day reserved for the "official" birthday celebrations. Perhaps you could try to institute this.

Halloween Party
If your birthday's close to 31 October, why not hijack the celebration and use it as your party theme?

What to wear:
As an alternative to an old sheet or a few bandages, try using a bit more imagination for your Halloween costume.
- Vampire Victim – wear a glamorous, long nightie and an eye-catching fake vampire wound (made from syrup and red food colouring, with two distinctive bite marks drawn on with a red marker pen). Attach a cardboard bat to your shoulder.
- The Grim Reaper – see if you can find a hooded cotton dressing-gown that can be adapted into the Grim Reaper's gown: make sure it's too big for you, remove the belt and dye it black if necessary. Dust it with some flour here and there. Wear a long, black dress underneath it and carry a cardboard scythe. Every so often, stand in the corner, pull your hood over your face and point at a victim of your choice.

- Horror Movie Victim – there's always an obvious victim in any horror movie. She's usually wearing smart, preppy clothes and sensible shoes, with her hair in a ponytail and an expression of wide-eyed innocence. Dress like this with the addition of a joke axe-in-the-head (these are available from any decent joke shop). Make some fake blood from syrup and red food colouring and drip this convincingly and gruesomely from your head wound.
- Ghost – wear old-fashioned clothes in grey, white or black, use white or grey make-up for any skin that's going to show, and dust your clothes and your hair with lots of flour.
- Macbeth's Witches – get together with two of your mates and plan a distinctive look. You don't have to wear pointy hats; perhaps you could be *glamorous* witches with lots of make-up, long black wigs and long, figure-hugging dresses. You'll need a cauldron – perhaps you could fill this with a chunk of dry ice and some gruesome ingredients (if you can't find eye of newt and wing of bat, make do with some rubber spiders, snakes and toads). Practise cackling.

Decorations:

Mood lighting is the key to an atmospheric Halloween party. Keep it dim and try replacing some of the ordinary light bulbs with coloured ones (this will probably wash out everyone's skin tone and make them look like zombies, which will tie in nicely with the Halloween theme). Buy a few glow-sticks and dot them about, too.

At least one pumpkin jack-o'-lantern is essential, but it's best to have more. They're pretty simple to make but pumpkins can be a bit tough, so be careful if you use a sharp knife. Take time over the design of your jack-o'-lantern face but keep it as simple as possible. Burn tea-lights or small candles inside the lanterns and place them strategically – one as the centrepiece on the food table should look good. (Don't waste the insides of the pumpkins after you've hollowed them out: use them to make pumpkin pie.)

You could make some paper streamers in ghost or bat shapes, or cut bat and spider shapes from black card and dangle them from the ceiling on lengths of cotton.

Food:
You can't have a Halloween party without some gruesome food. Here are a few ideas.
- Bogies on a Stick – bread sticks topped with melted cheese that's been given a splash of green food colouring.
- Witches' Fingers – frankfurters or sausages with a section cut out for the "fingernails"; use pieces of red, green or yellow pepper for these.
- Pus-filled Boils – make holes in cherry tomatoes, remove the pulp and fill them with cream cheese. Give them a little squeeze.
- Eyeballs – halve peeled, hard-boiled eggs, remove the yolks and replace them with cream cheese and a stuffed olive in the middle. To be even more revolting, you could dip a cocktail stick in red food colouring and use it to make the eyeballs bloodshot.
- Blood Punch – delicious Virgin Mary cocktail (see page 37) in a bowl. You could float some pieces of celery, cucumber or peppers cut to look like fingernails.

There are loads more themes you could choose for your party: movie stars, a colour code (e.g. black and white), James Bond, star signs, pop stars, Ancient Egypt or another historical period, your favourite TV series, cartoon characters, a masked ball. Or look at books, films and magazines for more ideas.

Dazzling Decorations

How does one achieve a party environment that says "tasteful, sophisticated and understated"? Or, alternatively, how do you make sure everyone knows they're attending a party held by the Queen of Cheese? Whatever look you're going for, choose from the two lists below (feel free to choose things from both of them) for party decoration ideas.

Cheesy and Charming

Parties are supposed to be fun, so don't hold back: find as many silly, tacky party decorations as you can.

Balloons

Use lots of them, attached to any blank space. Helium-filled ones are good (though be prepared for at least one of your friends to spend part of the evening talking in an amusing high-pitched voice).

Streamers and paper chains

Lots of these.

Banners

A nice big Happy Birthday banner looks good. Make your own, cutting out letters from a long strip of paper.

Fairy lights

Again, lots of these – you can't have too many.

Party poppers and party hooters

Leave bowls of these around for people to pick up and pop/hoot when they feel the urge.

Dazzling Decorations

Indoor sparklers
Hand out one or two of these to each guest at the door.

Glitter balls/revolving disco lights
If you can find or buy some, these will help set the tone nicely.

Lighting
You probably won't need any extra, what with all with the fairy lights, glitter balls, etc. But if you do, use a lamp or two, replacing ordinary lightbulbs with coloured ones.

Piñatas
Thought piñatas were just for little kids? Of course they're not! Try making this simple version yourself:

Piñatas

WHAT YOU NEED:
A large, fairly sturdy paper bag
Felt pens or paints and coloured tissue paper
Glue or tape
Scissors
String
Small sweets

WHAT YOU DO:
- Colour the paper bag with pens or paints.
- Cut fringes from tissue paper and attach them to the bag with glue.
- Cut longer fringes from tissue paper and attach them to the bottom of the bag with glue.
- Fill the bag halfway with small sweets. Seal it by folding down the top and securing it with tape or glue.

- Punch two holes in the top of the bag and thread it through with string.
- Hang up your piñatas and whack it with a rolled-up newspaper.

> ### Party Piñatas
> The piñata is a Mexican birthday tradition that's over three hundred years old. Unlike your paper bag creation, piñatas are usually made from papier mâché and shaped like animals. Traditionally, you're supposed to be blindfolded when you take a whack at the piñata.

Sophisticated and Stylish

This is the sort of party that takes itself a little bit more seriously. The key to a sophisticated party look is to have one or two main decorations (which should be classy, obviously) and very little else.

Balloons

Choose one or two colours and don't have too many. Helium-filled balloons look good attached to furniture with gift string – put some on the food table, too (but just a few).

Streamers and paper chains

Avoid like the plague. However, gift string pulled into spirals with a straight edge look great attached to balloons. Remember to colour coordinate.

Fairy lights

Since you're being classy and understated, some well-placed fairy lights could count as the main decoration. String them artistically on a wall, or around one or two door frames. There are lots of different kinds of fairy lights – some look a bit tacky.

Dazzling Decorations

Lighting
Use candles, tea-lights and a couple of lamps.

Banners
Avoid.

Glitter balls/revolving disco lights
No!

Flowers
Some vases of flowers, arranged beautifully, are perfect. Have three or four, and perhaps some sprigs of greenery dotted about. Paper flowers are veering towards the cheesy, but you could use them in a sophisticated sort of way. Here's how to make some.

Paper flowers

WHAT YOU NEED:
4 sheets of tissue paper measuring about 250 x 125 cm
Scissors
Cotton, thin string or wool

WHAT YOU DO:
- Put your four pieces of tissue paper on top of one another.
- With the short side towards you, fold about 1 cm up, then turn it over and fold 1 cm back – do this all the way up to make a concertina.
- Use scissors to round the edges on either end of your folded paper.
- Squeeze the middle and tie it with cotton.

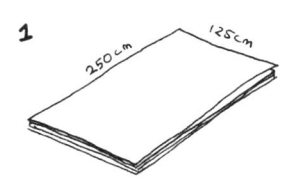

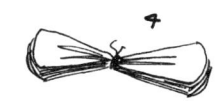

- Fan out the two sides.
- Gently and carefully separate the four layers of tissue paper. You have a flower.

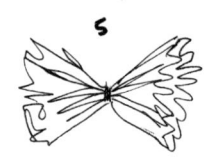

Tip: if the first one you do doesn't look very good, don't despair. Your third flower will look much better, once you've got the hang of it. You can join the flowers together to make chains, stick them in your hair (use a pipe cleaner round the middle instead of the cotton), dot them about in an artistic manner, etc.

Decorating Yourself – What to Wear

What about your own personal decoration? If it's a fancy dress party, you'll be going as the Bride of Frankenstein or Queen Victoria. But if not, you'll want to look extra special. The only golden rule is that you also want to be completely comfortable in your outfit: there's nothing worse than spending your party feeling self-conscious. It might be a good idea to get together with your friends and plan what each of you is going to wear – that way you can feel confident that you're not going to be massively over- or under-dressed, and that you're not going to be wearing the same top as your best mate!

It can be tempting to plaster on make-up in the hope that everyone will be stunned by your new glamorous appearance. But you run a high risk of ending up looking thirty-two and slightly orange – which might alarm your friends. It's probably a better idea to spend time having a relaxing bath, doing your nails, washing your hair and generally pampering yourself, and then putting on the amount of make-up you'd normally wear for a night out. Remember that young skin doesn't need much make-up, anyway.

> Birthday Bonanza
> For her twenty-first birthday, Paris Hilton threw five birthday parties — one each in Las Vegas, London, Hollywood, New York and Tokyo.

Food and Drink

What's your idea of party food? A couple of bowls of crisps, with a plate of Twiglets for that sophisticated look? If you're considering hosting a party where the only nutrition available is some stale crisps and flat lemonade, you need to read this.

Food Tips

✲ Making things yourself might sound like a lot of bother, but it's a lot cheaper than ready-made party food and usually tastes better, too.

✲ Plastic plates and cutlery will save you worrying about breaking things, and you can wash them up and re-use them at your next party!

✲ Put plates at either end of your food table so that people don't have to queue up to get their grub. If there are a lot of people and it's possible, try to have two food tables to avoid a scrum.

Fabulous Food

Posh party food is not difficult to make and isn't all that time-consuming (well, it is a bit – but it's all part of the pre-party fun). Get some of your friends to help you and you could even make this into a pre-party party, just for the inner circle – an exclusive group of between two and four. Afterwards, you and your friends can all go and get changed together and sit around sipping cocktails (more on those on page 36), feeling very pleased indeed with yourselves.

Here are a few ideas for party food that's easy to make and delicious to eat.

Garlic and Herb Bread

You can buy ready-made garlic bread in supermarkets that you just stick in the oven. But homemade does taste much nicer and it's pretty easy.

WHAT YOU NEED:
5 small French sticks
250 g butter, softened
10 –15 cloves of garlic, crushed
4–5 tbsp of fresh chopped herbs, such as parsley, oregano and thyme
Oven-proof silver foil

WHAT YOU DO:
- Pre-heat the oven to 200 ºC/Gas Mark 6.
- Mix the butter, garlic and herbs together well.
- Cut the bread into slices (but don't cut all the way through) and butter them with the garlic butter on both sides.
- Wrap the French sticks in foil and put them in the oven for 10 minutes.
- After 7 minutes, open up the foil then bake for another 3 minutes.
- Eat.

Cheese and Onion Tart

Make a couple of these, perhaps using a different type of cheese on each one.

WHAT YOU NEED:

200 g ready-made and ready-rolled puff pastry
(you'll find ready-made pastry in supermarkets –
though you might have to roll it out yourself)
50 g butter
6 medium-sized onions
100 g cheese – this can be any kind you like, but soft
cheeses work well

WHAT YOU DO:

- Pre-heat the oven to 220 ºC/Gas Mark 7.
- Chop the onions into fairly thick pieces. In a frying-pan, cook them over a low heat with the butter for about thirty minutes until they're really soft.
- Unroll your ready-rolled pastry or roll it out to about 30 cm by 30 cm, then lightly score a border 2 cm from the edges.
- Slice the cheese into small pieces and mix it with the onions, then put the mixture on top of the pastry within the border.
- Bake the tart in the oven for 15 – 20 minutes, or until golden.
- Cut it into squares and eat (it's nice cold as well as hot).

Perfect Pizzas

Again, it's good to have a few pizzas – try different toppings on each one.

WHAT YOU NEED:
Uncooked pizza bases (available in supermarkets)
Tomato purée or passata
Toppings: choose from mozzarella cheese, cheddar cheese, tomato slices, sliced mushrooms, olives, slices of pepperoni, fried chopped or sliced onion, fried or roasted green or red pepper, cooked sweetcorn, ham, part-cooked spinach or broccoli . . . or anything else you fancy.

WHAT YOU DO:
- Pre-heat the oven to the heat specified on the package of pizza bases.
- Spread a thin layer of tomato purée over the pizza bases.
- Choose some toppings – any combination you like – to put on.
- Put the pizzas in the oven for the length of time stated on the pizza base package.
- Cut into slices and eat.

Delicious Dips

Buy some houmous, tzatziki, guacamole or salsa, or make them yourself – look in cookery books and on the Internet for recipes. Then chop up some vegetables to use as dips – cucumber, red and green peppers, celery, carrots – and arrange them artistically. Pitta bread is also good for dipping – grill it until it's lightly browned, and then cut it into pieces.

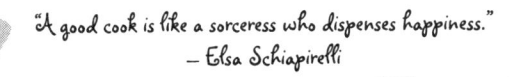

> "A good cook is like a sorceress who dispenses happiness."
> — Elsa Schiapirelli

Salads

Make two or three big salads with a combination of cherry tomatoes (if you use bigger tomatoes that you need to slice, put them in a separate bowl), lettuce, cucumber, avocados, celery, chopped carrot, radishes, spring onions and/or anything else you like. Dress the salads with some salt and pepper, olive oil and good vinegar (use about four times as much oil as vinegar) just before you serve them.

You might want to make a pasta or rice salad too.

Pasta Salad

WHAT YOU NEED:
300 g shaped pasta (e.g. shells, rings, bows, etc)
1 chopped red pepper
100 g chopped mushrooms
100 g cooked sweetcorn
50 g black olives
1 clove of garlic, crushed
Olive oil

WHAT YOU DO:
- Cook the pasta in boiling water according to the instructions on the packet, and then drain it and rinse it in cold water.
- Fry the pepper, mushrooms and sweetcorn with a clove of garlic in a splash of olive oil for about 5 minutes.
- Combine all the ingredients in a bowl.

Sweet Things

You could just stick to savoury food for your party, but it might be nice to include a fresh fruit salad, or just a bowl of apples, oranges and bananas for people to pick at. As a far less healthy option, put some Smarties, M&Ms or other sweets in bowls. If you want to be really extravagant, you could try . . .

Chocolate Strawberries

WHAT YOU NEED:
Strawberries – enough for everyone to have a taste
A few large bars of good-quality plain chocolate

WHAT YOU DO:
- Heat a saucepan of water. When it starts to boil, reduce it to a simmer.
- Stand a heat-proof bowl on top of the saucepan. Break the chocolate into pieces and heat until it's melted. It's important not to let the water boil, or the chocolate will get overheated and become lumpy.
- Arrange the strawberries on paper towels, pointing upwards.
- Take the bowl off the heat and spoon some melted chocolate over each strawberry. This can be messy.
- Leave the fruit to dry.
- Arrange the strawberries on a plate and eat them. You'll find that however many of these you make, there won't be enough.

Delicious Drinks

You don't want your guests to be staggering about and slurring, so it's best to avoid alcohol altogether. But it doesn't mean that you can't sip exotic cocktails . . .

Each recipe will make enough for two cocktails. Simply mix the ingredients together – in a cocktail shaker, if possible, to look extra posh.

Virgin Mary

400 ml tomato juice
Dash of Worcestershire sauce
Dash of Tabasco sauce
Pinch of pepper
Celery sticks (if you like)

Gentle Sea Breeze

300 ml cranberry juice
150 ml grapefruit juice
Crushed ice

Carrot, Apple and Honey Drink

400 ml carrot juice
100 ml apple juice
2–3 tsp of honey

Fruity Yoghurt

Use a blender for this one.

100 g raspberries, strawberries or
  another soft fruit of your choice
150 ml plain yoghurt
300 ml cold milk

Sunrise

300 ml orange juice mixed with 50 ml lime juice
50 ml grenadine (pour this into the serving glasses first, and don't stir the drink)

Coffee Milk Shake

Use a blender.

3 tsp instant coffee powder
1 tsp sugar
500 ml cold milk
4 ice cubes
1 drop vanilla essence

You probably won't want to go to the effort of making posh cocktails all evening, so make sure you have a few other soft drinks, including fizzy water, orange juice and lemonade. And you might want to provide a huge bowl of punch – try one of these:

Pink Punch

WHAT YOU NEED:
1.5 litres cranberry juice
1.5 litres white grape juice
200 ml lemonade
750 ml fizzy water

WHAT YOU DO:
Just combine all the ingredients and serve with a ladle from a big punch bowl. There's enough for about thirty people.

Hawaiian Fruit Punch

WHAT YOU NEED:
12 strawberries, sliced
3 oranges, sliced
The juice of 4 lemons
1 litre grape juice
1.5 litres lemonade
1 litre orange juice

WHAT YOU DO:
Mix all of the ingredients together in a large bowl and serve with a ladle.

Hot Punch

WHAT YOU NEED:
A very large (more than 3 litre) saucepan
1.5 litres boiling water
500 ml apple juice
500 ml orange juice
500 ml pineapple juice
2 large washed lemons
100 g sugar cubes
Pinch of ground cinnamon
Pinch of grated nutmeg
Pinch of ground cloves

WHAT YOU DO:
- Rub the sugar cubes on the rinds of the washed lemons. This will rub the zest onto the sugar. Then crush the cubes in a saucepan.
- Add the spices, boiling water and fruit juices.

- Heat the mixture gently but don't boil it.
- Squeeze both the lemons and put the juice into a heat-proof punch bowl.
- Add the hot liquid.
- Serve – it's enough for about twenty people to have a small cup.

Party Games

It's always a good idea to have plenty of games thought out in advance before your party. They can break the ice and get people talking to one another, they're fun, and they're a great excuse for flirting. You might not feel like playing all of them, or one might prove so popular that you don't have time for any others, but think of five or six games to play before the party and you shouldn't run out of ideas.

Some of them need a bit of preparation, but the games listed here are all simple to play and (hopefully) great fun. They're also all very silly, but that's the whole point of birthday-party games. To start with, here are a few old favourites that you might well know already . . .

Pass the Orange

A great game for getting up close and personal with your guests. Everyone forms a circle. An orange is passed from person to person in the crook of their chins. Anyone who drops the orange is out, until there's only one person left. (The winner should get a prize – try to think of something better than a bruised orange.)

Spin the Bottle

Yes, it's corny and yes, it can be excruciatingly embarrassing. In case you don't already know, the idea is to put an empty bottle on its side in the middle of the floor. Everyone sits around it in a circle. One person spins the bottle. When it stops spinning, whoever the neck of the bottle is pointing at has to kiss the spinner. Sometimes it's best to work out what sort of kiss you have to do! Then the kisser takes his or her turn to spin . . . and so on, until no one can take any more excitement/embarrassment/snogging.

Truth, Dare, Kiss or Promise

Look on page 57 – 58 for a bursting balloons version of this game and some suggestions for dares. The person who begins asks the next person "Truth, Dare, Kiss or Promise". If they reply 'Truth', ask them a question that they must tell the truth to. If they answer 'Dare', dare them to do something fun, etc. Remember to take turns and keep whatever is said or done a secret!

If you're thinking of being a bit more adventurous, why not try these not-so-well-known party games . . .

Musical Clothes

This is a bit like musical chairs, except everyone ends up looking really stupid. It takes a bit of preparation but it's worth it. You need a big bag or bin liner full of old clothes – hats, coats, bras, jumpers, T-shirts – anything you can find, the more geeky the better. It might be worth spending a few pounds at a charity shop for some really choice items. Someone is designated to control the music. Everyone else sits in a circle. When the music starts, the bag is passed from person to person. When the music stops, the person holding the bag has to delve into it and put on the first item of clothing they touch. When all the clothes in the bag have been used up, it's time for the music controller to make a judgement on who looks the silliest. The winner gets a prize.

Frozen T-Shirts

A very silly game that will need some advance preparation. Players try to put on T-shirts that have been dampened, folded and put in the freezer overnight. You then try various methods of thawing them out – sitting on them, breathing on them, etc. The person who gets his or her T-shirt on first is the winner.

The Ice Cream Game

Put a big tub of ice cream and lots of spoons on a table, and gather together a pile of silly clothes, such as wellies, ski goggles and an old coat and hat. Everyone sits in a circle and rolls a dice. When someone rolls a six, they have to put on all the silly clothes and eat as much ice cream as they can before another person rolls a six. That person does the same, and so on until the tub is empty.

Stacking Up

This is a good game for introducing people to one another – by making them sit on one another's laps! (Well, it's a direct approach.) Don't shy away from being the Question Master: if you're good at logic problems, you'll have great fun working out how to get your friend sitting on the lap of the person she fancies.

Everyone sits on chairs in a circle, except for the Question Master. The Question Master asks a question of the whole group: anyone who answers "yes" to the question has to move one place to his or her right – whether there's already someone sitting there or not. The Question Master continues asking questions until no one can take any more. It's best to ask questions about things that can be easily verified – for example, if you ask "Is blue your favourite colour?" people might only

answer "yes" if they want to move to their right. Some examples of questions:
- Do you have brown eyes?
- Are you wearing jeans?
- Do you live in [insert name of a town area]?
- Do you go to [insert name of school]?
- Is your name [insert name here – if you want to be obvious!]?

Messy Bobbing

If you don't mind behaving like a pre-schooler and losing any vestiges of sophistication or dignity, try this game: Fill several bowls (or one big bowl) with water and float one apple per person. (You might have to divide into groups and have several rounds.) In time-honoured Halloween fashion, everyone has to try to grab an apple using only their teeth. Then, the second someone's been successful, everyone has to bob for marshmallows in large bowls filled with flour. Have your camera ready for the end.

> An Apple Bobbing Superstition
> The winner of a game of apple bobbing is supposed to be the first person to get married.

The Psychiatrist

Someone is chosen or volunteers to be the Psychiatrist. He or she has to leave the room until called back in. While the Psychiatrist is out of earshot, everyone else has to decide what strange psychological problem they all share. For example, everyone could:
- be frightened of balloons
- have to shout "Knickers!" whenever a particular person is mentioned

- have a compulsion to eat peanuts whenever someone says "party"
- be secretly in love with the Psychiatrist
- have lost their memory for the last twenty-four hours
- violently dislike the person on their left.

The Psychiatrist asks everyone a question in turn and struggles to make a diagnosis.

I've Never Done That

This is a game that can out people's secrets – if they're honest, that is. You need ten or so tokens for each player – ideally these will be food of some sort, like jelly beans, Smarties or chocolates, for example. Everyone sits in a circle and takes it in turns to say something they've never done. Anyone who *has* done it has to eat one of his or her tokens. The end of the game is when only one person has any tokens left. You can play this game tactically, and get some hilarious results. A few examples:

- I've never snogged [insert name of your choice here].
  (That's if you really want to embarrass someone – and, you never know, maybe six people will have to eat a token.)
- I've never been to France.
  (As a way of getting everyone else to eat their tokens – but only if most people in the room have been to France and you haven't, of course!)
- I've never fancied a teacher.
  (How honest are your friends?)

> "You can tell a lot about a fellow's character from his way of eating jelly beans."
> – Ronald Reagan, former US President

Great Mates Quiz

Compile twenty or so questions about your friends, then have a quiz to find out how well you all know one another (this will only work if it's a fairly small group who all know each other quite well – it's not going to be fair otherwise). For example:

- Whose middle name is Dorothea/Algernon/Rainbow?
- Which person was born in Glasgow/Skegness/Australia?
- Whose mum plays the saxophone/golf/for Arsenal?
- Who lost her bikini top when she dived off the top board?

> Did you know that in a group of twenty-five people or more, the chances are that two of you will share a birthday? (This can be explained with maths, but this is a book about birthdays, so let's not go there.) So you might well have a friend you can get together with for a shared birthday treat.

If you need some more games ideas, have a look at some of the games for sleepovers on page 57.

Happy Families

You'll want your parents to spend the party evening in Peru, *they'll* want to spend it hovering anxiously two centimetres from your elbow. But compromise is possible, and both you and your worry-wart parents can be satisfied if you have a long and exhaustive talk about all the issues and come to some agreements beforehand.

You don't want your mum standing menacingly at the door turning away anyone in trainers. Nor do you want her or your dad swanning around smiling and introducing people as if this were *their* party (the cheek!). However, if the party's at your home, remember that it's *their* home too, so it's understandable that a) they're used to being the hosts and b) they're worried that it's going to end up full of cigarette butts and smelling of cheap cider and sick. They will need convincing that you have planned a sophisticated gathering of the social elite. Here's how:

- Show the guest list to your mum or dad, explaining who everyone is if necessary. Agree on a certain number of people – between twenty and thirty will probably keep both of you happy.
- Explain that their beautiful home will remain a haven of style, luxury and taste. Well, at least it won't look any different from the way it does now. Agree to do all or most of the preparation yourself, and all or most of the clearing up yourself. The preparation could include putting any favourite breakable things in a safe place where no harm can come to them, taking up any rugs that are especially precious, and maybe covering the sofa with a nice throw or two. Beware of making the place look like a padded cell, though – you want to make the party look welcoming to your lovely friends, not like the venue for a food fight. Draw the line if your parents suggest covering everything in plastic sheeting.
- Agree a start and end time for the party with your parents, and make sure your guests know about it.
- Make some rules about what your parents' role will be. You don't want them standing in the party room with their hands on their hips scrutinising people *or* getting too friendly – tell them gently that you'd like this to be your party and for them to keep a low profile: their place is out of the way, sipping a glass of wine and keeping quiet. They should understand. Assure them that you'll let them know at the very first sign of any trouble (which there won't be, of course, but your parents will be desperate for reassurance).

- Agree to tell the neighbours about the party – or your mum or dad could do this if they'd rather. Give the neighbours at least a week's notice, so they can make themselves scarce if they want to. It's best to go round and tell them in person (the neighbours will think that you are mature and trustworthy if you do this . . . the fools).
- Agree on the music volume. Test this out by standing outside the house, or even next door if you're very friendly with your neighbours.
- Agree an alcohol policy. It's probably best not to serve any alcohol at your party – not that you or any of your wonderful, sensible mates would ever do anything stupid, but you don't want to run the risk of anyone lurching about, throwing up and frightening the cat. And apart from anything else, it will make your parents happy. Make sure everyone knows what the policy is on alcohol and smoking (which you'll definitely want to ban or your home will smell like an ashtray for months).

Delightful Little Brothers and Sisters

Younger brothers and sisters bring nothing but joy and loveliness, of course. Well, some of the time. At your party, depending on their age and number, they might have a tendency to want to hide your CDs, booby-trap the decorations, set their hamster loose on the food table or drink all the coke and embark on a sugar-fuelled path of general destruction. If this is in any way likely to be the case, a serious chat is in order. You could promise your little brother or sister a reward if they behave themselves – offer to take them to a movie or for a pizza. And let them know that there will be serious consequences if they misbehave – enlist the help of your parents for this. It might even be best if your younger siblings spend the evening at a friend's or relative's, but let your mum and dad decide about that.

Chapter 2
BIRTHDAY TREATS, SLEEPOVERS AND SURPRISES

As well as getting birthday cards, presents and maybe having a party, everyone deserves a bit of extra pampering on their birthday. You might want to spoil someone rotten on their special day, or you might want to pamper yourself on your own birthday. Either way, with a bit of ingenuity and without breaking the bank, you can make it a day to remember.

Birthday Treats

If you're giving someone a birthday treat, make sure you do something that you know they'll like, rather than something you'd like yourself! (It's amazing how you can fool yourself into thinking your dad would love a candle-lit bubble bath and a makeover.) Here are some ideas.

Breakfast in Bed

This is an especially good idea for your mum or dad. Make sure you decorate the tray – it might be nice to include the person's birth flower (this will be easier in some months than in others), use napkins and the best crockery and glasses. Line the tray with a pretty tea towel (this will make things less likely to fall over). Here are some ideas for a delicious birthday breakfast tray.

For a health freak
Fruit juice, muesli in a bowl, a jug of semi-skimmed milk, a pot of herbal tea, a freshly prepared fruit salad (or just a piece of fruit or two).

An indulgently sweet breakfast
A Danish pastry or doughnut, a jug of milk, a pot of tea or coffee, a croissant with butter and little pots of jam.

A fry-up
(Well, it *is* their birthday . . .) A plate of grilled bacon, grilled sausage, fried or scrambled egg, grilled tomato and/or baked beans. Vegetarians can be unhealthy, too – give them fried or scrambled egg, grilled tomato, fried mushrooms, baked beans and maybe a vegetarian sausage. Don't forget a cup of tea or coffee, and make sure it's all piping hot when you serve it.

Plain and simple
A few pieces of freshly made toast just the way they like it, with a dish of butter or margarine, Marmite, and little pots of jam, marmalade and honey (give them a choice, or just their favourite). Add a pot of tea or coffee with some milk. Include some fruit juice, too.

Pamper a Pal
Invite a friend to an afternoon of birthday pampering, which might include beauty treatments, make-up and hair styling. The idea of the process is that your friend ends up looking and feeling fabulous, so *don't* use her as a guinea pig for some strange-sounding hair treatments or make-up effects you've heard about. In fact, only subject your friend to your make-up or hair-styling skills if you're especially good at it: the end result should be that she looks fabulous, not like a

Birthday Treats

fashion victim from a bygone era who's been given an electric shock. A group of you could get together and do this for your friend, with each of you offering your specialist skills. Here are some ideas for a pampering afternoon:

- Run your friend a luxurious bubble bath surrounded by candles. Leave her a selection of her favourite magazines to flick through as she soaks. Provide her with her favourite drink and leave her alone – you can be preparing beauty treatments.
- Make a simple face-pack for practically no cost. Mix 3 dessertspoons of powdered oats with enough honey to make a paste. (Grind the oats with a pestle and mortar to powder them.) Then apply the face-pack to your friend's skin – use gentle circular movements as you apply it. Avoid the eye area: put a slice of cucumber over each eye instead. Leave your friend to relax for about twenty minutes (maybe while she's in the bath), then wash it off. It'll be messy, but your friend's skin should feel lovely. (Try this yourself first to make sure you agree.) When the skin's clean, apply some light moisturiser – whichever kind your friend is used to is best.
- Give your friend a home-made hair treatment. For example: after shampooing, dissolve a teaspoon of honey in a litre of water and use this to give the hair a final rinse (don't wash it out); mix 2 egg yolks with 1 – 2 tbsp of water and leave in as a conditioner for 15 minutes, then rinse out completely; or use a whole egg and a little lemon juice as a conditioner – again, leave for 15 – 20 minutes.

> "Beauty is in the eye of the beholder and it may be necessary from time to time to give a stupid or misinformed beholder a black eye."
> – Miss Piggy (from The Muppet Show)

Shopping Trip

Take your friend shopping for clothes (she might well have some birthday money to spend) and offer helpful advice on her outfits (if she wants it, that is!). This is *her* shopping trip, so let her decide which shops she wants to visit and don't get impatient about how long she wants to spend in each one.

Birthday Cake

Make the birthday boy or girl a birthday cake (see page 87– 97 for some recipes). Present it to them in a box tied with a ribbon. Even if the cake's not absolutely perfect, they'll be bound to love this.

Birthday Outings

Whether it's your birthday or someone else's, it can be great fun to get a group of your friends together for some kind of special outing. If it's for a friend, make sure you talk to them first and find out the kind of thing they want to do. Here are a few ideas.

Bathing Belles

If you're lucky enough to live near a beach or an open-air swimming pool and it's the summertime, invite all your mates for a great birthday treat. Organise games of water polo or just laze in the sun. Take along plenty of waterproof sun protection.

Ice-skating Extravaganza

No one has to be an expert to have fun ice skating – even if you've never been before, you should just about be able to stagger round looking inelegant after falling on your bum a few times.

On Your Bike

If you and your mates are keen cyclists, suggest getting together for a day's bike ride. Work out your route and find somewhere good to stop for lunch (you could all bring a packed lunch). Make the route fairly challenging, and then organise somewhere to relax afterwards with tea and cake.

Al Fresco Afternoon

A picnic is more low-key than a party but can be just as much fun (plus the clearing up isn't nearly such hard work). Take some big blankets or sarongs to spread on the ground (and you might need to put down some plastic sheets if the ground's wet). Instead of boring sandwiches and packets of crisps, take some home-made pasta or rice salad (see page 35 for a recipe), some plain grilled chicken, slices of ham, tomatoes, houmous, pitta bread and French bread for people to make their own sandwiches. Chop up some carrots, celery and peppers to dip into houmous or other dips (like tzatziki or salsa). Paper plates are lighter to carry, but plastic plates are a bit more environmentally friendly as you can take them home, wash them up and use them again. Take some outdoor games with you, such as badminton racquets and shuttlecocks, plus a length of rope to tie between two trees as a net (or don't bother with a net); a frisbee; a skipping rope (see how many skipping rhymes you can remember from when you were eight). If there are enough of you, you could play all the playground games you thought you'd grown out of (but you will find they are even better fun now). Or, try this silly outdoor game:

Cotton-ball and Spoon Race

- Divide everyone into three or four teams and make sure there's one spoon per team.
- Place one big bowl (e.g. a washing-up bowl) of cotton-balls for each team on the ground. Some distance away (maybe ten metres) place an empty bowl for each team.
- One person from each team picks up a cotton-ball in their spoon and tries to get it into the empty bowl as quickly as

possible (without touching it). If they drop the cotton-ball, they have to leave it and go back for another one.
- When all the cotton-balls are either in the bowls at the far end of the course or on the ground, the team with the most cotton-balls in its bowl is declared the winner.

Unless you're going to be near other picnickers, take along a small CD player and plenty of music or an MP3 player and speakers. If you plan a picnic and when the day comes it's pouring with rain, don't despair: move all of the furniture out of one of the rooms in your house, lay down some rugs on the floor and have your picnic there. You might not be able to play badminton, but you could get out Twister instead.

Team Treat
If you're a sports fan, go to a football match or another game with a group of your friends. Afterwards, go back to your place to celebrate/discuss where your team was badly let down by poor management, injuries, the weather, etc.

Behind the Wheel
Get a group of you together and go quad-biking or go-karting. This can be expensive, but it's great fun if you and your mates can afford it.

Fashion Fun
Have a shopping-fest (including planned breaks where you all meet up for a drink and a natter). Afterwards, everyone goes back to your place where you set up a catwalk for your friends to model their purchases.

> "Hold a true friend with both your hands."
> — Nigerian Proverb

Birthday Sleepovers

If you want a birthday celebration with just your best mates, you can't do better than a sleepover.

Ten Top Sleepover Tips

1. You can only have a limited number of people at a sleepover — think about how many people you can comfortably fit in the room you'll be sleeping in. If you're worried about offending friends because you're going to leave them out, plan a different birthday treat instead, like a picnic, where you can invite more people.
2. When everyone arrives, check that they have everything they need with them (pyjamas, wash bag, sleeping bag, etc) — it's better than finding out someone's left their toothbrush at home when there's no time to do anything about it.
3. If anyone has to sleep on the floor, everyone has to — you can't have some people with comfy beds and sofas and others without.
4. Have a word with your parents to make sure they don't burst through the door every five minutes with some obvious excuse. Sleepovers are for sharing innermost secrets and serious gossip — the sudden appearance of your mother bearing a tray of teacakes can ruin the moment. Enlist your parents' help to make sure any little brothers or sisters don't cause mayhem.

5. Make sure there's at least one camera to record the evening.
6. Have plenty of games lined up.
7. Make sure there are plenty of snacks for everyone – check that the food is OK for everyone to eat (some people might be vegetarian or have food allergies, etc).
8. Make sure you have enough breakfast food for everyone in the morning.
9. Rent one or two movies – you don't have to watch them but they'll be handy if everyone feels like slumping.
10. Have plenty of CDs lined up – including some atmospheric background music for ghost stories.

Pyjama Food

Have a look at the food ideas on pages 31 to 37. The best food for sleepovers is the kind you can eat while lying around on the floor or slumping on a sofa – this includes:

- Popcorn – essential for movie watching, of course. Make your own in the microwave or in a saucepan (with some butter and salt, or sugar if you'd rather).
- Dips – you can make your own or buy some houmous, tzatziki, guacamole or salsa. Dip in pieces of grilled pitta bread and chopped-up carrots, celery, cucumber and red and green peppers.
- Garlic bread.
- Sausage rolls. You can buy them or make your own in advance and freeze them uncooked – put them in the oven on the night of the sleepover. Don't forget you can make vegetarian sausage rolls – instead of sausagemeat you can use a mixture of cheese, onion and breadcrumbs.
- Bowls of nuts and raisins.
- Olives.
- Savoury or sweet scones and muffins.

You could also have bowls of crisps, chocolate bars, Smarties or

M&Ms. Look on page 38 for some drinks to make – the cocktails are good to try when there are just a few of you, and you could ask each person to bring a different cocktail ingredient. Don't forget to supply plenty of kitchen roll or napkins for anything messy.

> "One cannot think well, love well, sleep well, if one has not dined well."
> – Virginia Woolf, writer

For breakfast you'll probably want to keep things as simple as possible – but don't forget it altogether (it's quite easy to do this). Offer your friends one or two different cereals (make sure you've stocked up on milk), some fruit, and toast or croissants with jam, marmalade, honey or Marmite.

Silly Games

It's good to have some games ready in advance – you might not feel like or get around to playing all of them, but it's better than running out. There are some games you could play on pages 40 to 45, but sleepovers are a chance to be really silly (these are just your best mates, after all). Here are a few daft ideas.

Burst a Balloon and Do a Dare

Write some dares on pieces of paper, such as:
- do a handstand
- wear a pair of knickers on your head for the rest of the evening (maybe best to have a few clean and non-embarrassing pairs available for this)
- dance the Dance of the Seven Veils using tea towels
- do an impression of a chimp

- hum the National Anthem without laughing
- put two ice cubes down your top
- take off your socks and wear one on each ear
- perform a ballet dance
- sing "I'm a Little Teapot" and do all the actions.

When you've written all your dares, roll up the pieces of paper, put them inside un-blown-up balloons, then blow them up. Players have to burst a balloon, then do the dare inside. If you like, you could make this into a game of Truth or Dare and add some "truth" questions inside the balloons – but be careful with your questions so that no one will get upset.

> Sing "Happy Birthday to You" in German:
> Zum Geburtstag viel Gluck
> Zum Geburtstag viel Gluck
> Zum Geburtstag viel Gluck
> Zum Geburtstag viel Gluck

Torchlight Limbo

Turn off all the lights and use a torch beam to limbo underneath. Start off with the torch a metre or so from the ground then gradually lower it – you can take turns to hold the torch or put it on top of furniture or boxes (this will make sure it's the same height for everyone).

Karaoke

It's cheesy, it's often painful and it's nearly always completely appalling. But you know you want to.

Pin the Handbag on the Celebrity

Search newspapers and magazines for a big picture of a famous person holding some kind of accessory – this could be a handbag, a small dog, a hat, etc. Cut off the picture of the accessory, then pin or blu-tak the celebrity to a board. Add some blu-tak to the accessory. The idea is exactly the same as Pin the Tail on the Donkey and just as silly.

Which Would You Rather?

Everyone takes it in turns to ask one other person which of two dreadful things they would rather do. It sounds simple but will have hilarious results. For instance:

Which would you rather . . .
- eat a woodlouse or snog [insert boy's name of your choice here]?
- run through the school naked or drink from a toilet bowl?
- moon the headteacher or spend the night in a haunted house?

Makeover From Hell

Provide a variety of (cheap or least favourite) lipsticks, eyeliners, blusher, mascara, etc. (You could ask everyone to bring some make-up for this but warn them not to bring their best stuff.) Everyone has to make up their own face without the aid of a mirror. The ghastliest result is the winner. Make sure you have a camera handy to capture the horrible consequences of this game.

The Handbag Game

This game is better with lots of people. Everyone takes two items from her handbag and puts them in "the Mystery Bag" (an empty handbag) without the others seeing. Items are removed one by one and everyone has to guess which mystery item belongs to which person.

Twister
This game was fun when you were six and it's just as much fun now.

> "No party is any fun unless seasoned with folly."
> — Desiderius Erasmus

Sleepover Essentials

- Give each other a manicure. Divide into pairs and do one another's nails. Make sure there's plenty of different coloured nail varnish.
- Try out beauty treatments (you could try some of the home-made ones on page 51).
- Do one another's hair.
- Give each other a makeover. (This might be a good idea after you've finished the Makeover From Hell on the previous page.)
- Tell ghost stories. When you're all settled in your sleeping bags, everyone tells the spookiest story they've ever heard. Play some creepy background music, turn off the lights and prepare to be terrified.

> "Life is nothing without friendship."
> — Cicero, Ancient Roman

Sleepover Souvenirs

A sleepover souvenir T-shirt is a good way to remember a birthday sleepover. Have enough plain white T-shirts for everyone and some fabric pens. Each person writes or draws something on all the T-shirts. When they've finished, there's a unique, stylish item of clothing for everyone to take away. You might even want to wear them – though probably not in public. (You could do this with pillowcases, too.)

Birthday Surprises

Before you rush off and quickly organise a surprise party for your best friend – wait! Come back, sit down and concentrate for a minute. Birthday surprises are notoriously difficult to get right, and you don't want your mate running away in floods of tears/refusing to speak to you for six months/completely missing his or her own party. Here are a few pointers to start off with.

Top Ten Tips for Surprise Birthdays

1. **Limit the number of people who are in on the surprise.**
   The possibility of the secret getting out rises in direct proportion to number of people who know about it. (We could express this in a maths formula . . . but let's not.)

2. **Don't tell anyone who is likely to blab.**
   We all have friends who are blabbers. You know it, they know it – they are genetically incapable of keeping a secret. They will probably know themselves well enough to understand why you couldn't tell them about the surprise in advance. (What with the word "surprise" being a key element.) But do make sure that they're a big part of the celebrations once the secret's out, to let them know they're appreciated for other things. And *don't* tell any little kids about the surprise – they will definitely blab.

3. **Make sure the person you're surprising likes surprises.**
   Some people *hate* surprises. Make sure your friend isn't one of them.

4. ***Make sure the surprise is something your friend will enjoy.***
   It doesn't have to be a surprise party (shy people might not enjoy that) – you could have a surprise sleepover, trip to the beach, picnic, day of pampering . . . Some people would be embarrassed at being the centre of attention in a large group. Make sure you choose your surprise to suit the birthday person.

5. ***Don't let your friend feel miserable because s/he thinks everyone's forgotten.***
   Let your friend know you haven't forgotten their birthday and tell them about some kind of low-key "screening activity" (like coming over to your place to celebrate with some flat lemonade and a plate of Twiglets) so that you can spring your surprise – more on that later.

6. ***Are you the right person to spring the surprise?***
   If you're going to organise a birthday surprise for a friend, you need to be a good actor. In fact, you need to be able to lie convincingly over a period of time. You must be constantly alert and keep arrangements hidden (e.g. party food and drink, suspicious packets of balloons, etc). Are you sure you're up to it? If not, find another close friend for the job and help them plan it, but let them do the talking.

7. ***Make sure the guest list is the birthday girl or boy's and not yours.***
   For example, don't invite anyone you know very well but they don't, don't invite someone just because *you* fancy them, etc.

8. ***Make sure that the birthday boy or girl hasn't made other plans.***
   After all, there's nothing worse than having a birthday surprise without the person whose birthday you're celebrating. You will feel a bit silly. See advice on this later on.

9. ***Only meet with your co-conspirators when you're sure the birthday boy or girl isn't going to turn up.***
   If the birthday girl or boy sees you all whispering together in a huddle but isn't allowed to join in, they will be a) highly suspicious and/or b) hurt and upset.

10. ***Remember that the object of the surprise is to give your friend a lovely time on their birthday.***
    The object of the surprise is *not* simply to terrify them or to give everyone else a good time. Make sure you do things during the party (or other event) that are personal, appropriate and special to the birthday boy or girl – there are some ideas later.

> "Nearly all the best things that came to me in life have been unexpected."
> — Carl Sandberg, poet

Organising a Birthday Surprise

Now that we have a few basics out of the way, we can get down to the nitty gritty of surprise: organisation.

Undercover Ops

Organising a surprise is not easy. Be prepared to let your role as organiser become a full-time job. You have to be on the alert at all times to stop the secret from getting out, or in case a key element of your plan goes wrong (something almost certainly *will* go wrong, so make contingency plans and allow yourself time to put them into practice). The event will only go smoothly if you've put a lot of thought and planning into it. Be aware of this before you start – if you're not going to put in the effort, it could turn into a disaster.

The Surprise and the Smoke Screen

All of the aforementioned Top Ten Tips are important, but the two really crucial factors are 1) that the surprise is something your friend will love, and 2) that s/he doesn't find out about it. First of all, decide what your friend would most like to do on his or her birthday, and work out how you can make it happen – or make do with something almost as good. For example, your friend's idea of a great birthday might be dinner with Brad Pitt followed by a wild party with all her mates (and Brad). She might have to make do with just the party (without Brad) – but you could organise some Brad-related presents, including a cardboard cut-out of the man himself if possible. And don't forget to add some special extras that he or she would never have thought of – see below for some ideas. Next, think of something that the birthday girl or boy would *quite* like to do, just involving a couple of mates: for example, going for a pizza, or seeing a movie, or both, with you and another friend. This will be your "screening activity" – i.e. what your friend *thinks* she's doing for her birthday – so that she doesn't make any other plans. You must make sure that the screening activity isn't too disappointing, and also that it isn't something he or she would rather be doing! Only once you're sure your friend is available should you start organising the *real* event.

Bad Birthday Boy!

On his thirtieth birthday, Keanu Reeves's friends threw a surprise party for him. He thought he was going to a hockey match and, when he realised what was really going on, he reacted rather badly – he mooned his guests.

Shhhhh!
Make sure all the people on the guest list are invited well in advance, and make absolutely sure they know that it's a secret! Emblazon this on the front of your invitation. Maybe something along the lines of . . .

TOP SECRET
You are invited to a SURPRISE party for Lily at 7 p.m. EXACTLY, 10 September at 22 Alpha House. DO NOT breathe a word about it to anyone (except Karen, Mo, Jess, Matty, Mark and Kat) under PAIN OF DEATH. Tell KAT if you can come (NOT LILY!!) as soon as you can.

Top Secret Teamwork
You can ask your close friends to help you with the organising – perhaps a few people could each bring some food and drink, one or two people could bring some decorations, one person could be in charge of organising the music, and someone else could design and make a Happy Birthday banner or poster (perhaps with a blown-up photo of the birthday boy or girl). Of course, make sure everyone gets to the venue before the friend you're surprising.

Synchronise Watches . . .
If you're planning a surprise party in someone's house (a friend's or the birthday girl's) you'll need to make sure the relevant adults are involved and you'll also need a good excuse to keep the birthday boy or girl away from the house for a few hours before the party. Perhaps another friend could take her to have a manicure or a pizza or some other birthday treat. But make sure they're not going to turn up at the house where the party preparations are in full swing. Leave yourselves at least three hours to get everything ready.

The guests should arrive at the party (or picnic, or sleepover, etc) at least half an hour before the birthday girl or boy. Make sure everyone knows that they can't be late, and that they should all have a present and card. They will have to have some kind of advance warning that your friend is about to arrive (either with you or another friend who is supposed to be involved in the screening activity) – maybe you could send a quick text, or someone could act as a look-out. When the birthday girl or boy arrives, hopefully it will be a *big* surprise. The second the door opens, everyone could burst into a tuneful rendition of "Happy Birthday To You" (with four-part harmonies, obviously) or simply shout "Happy Birthday!" followed by huge cheers and hugs and kisses. You will soon be able to tell whether the enormous and time-consuming effort of organising the surprise was worth it – if you've followed all the tips, it should be!

A Special Song
"Happy Birthday to You" is one of the three most popular songs in the English language. The other two are "Auld Lang Syne" and "For He's a Jolly Good Fellow".

Life Story
Whatever surprise event you've planned, make it really special by giving your friend some extra surprises that are personal to him or her. Look at the present ideas on pages 72 – 80 and think about making a song-per-year CD, a special framed photo, a birthday document or a Birthday Box, and perhaps a collage card (see page 81). If it's a landmark birthday like a sixteenth, you might want to go completely crazy and organise a Life Story moment for your mate.

Make a Life Story Moment

WHAT YOU NEED:
Some key people from your friend's life – e.g. granny, mum and dad, friends, someone who can impersonate a particular teacher (a teacher at a surprise event might be *too* much of a surprise)
A chair for your friend
A screen for people to hide behind
Photos
Some method of displaying the photos (digital photos displayed on a computer screen would be ideal, but a whiteboard with photos stuck to it at appropriate moments, till at the end it's full, would do just as well)
Any relevant music
A photo album or posh scrap-book
A typed-up version of your script

WHAT YOU DO:
- Write a script. You or another friend will play the role of the narrator and read out a script to your friend's life up until now. Sort out which people and photos you have from key moments in your friend's life and incorporate them into it. (There's a short example of the kind of thing on the next page.)
- Organise the key people you're going to mention, and get them to say a few words before leaping out from behind the screen to lots of emotional hugging and kissing. It totally doesn't matter if the people concerned have already seen the birthday boy or girl – it will still be funny. Display photos and play music wherever relevant.

- At the end, when you're up to date with your friend's illustrious and eventful life, give them their special Life Story book. It will have a typed-up version of the script, together with photos – you could even include newspaper headlines from key moments (or make up your own newspaper headlines) or add cut-outs from magazines. You might want to do the whole thing electronically rather than sticking in photographs.

FOR EXAMPLE, YOUR SCRIPT COULD START OFF LIKE THIS:
Narrator: Lily Burnard, ace swimmer, cordon-bleu cook and maths whiz, tonight, THIS IS YOUR LIFE STORY!
(Cue music – perhaps her favourite track of the moment, or another relevant song. Sit your guest of honour in the special chair.)
Lily, you were born in Manchester General Hospital at 3.14 a.m. Your mum and dad were overjoyed!
(Cue photo of Lily as a baby.)
Mum: Yes, Lily, you were a beautiful baby! *(Or whatever slushy stuff Lily's mum comes up with. Mum enters from behind screen amid scenes of weeping, great joy, etc.)*
Narrator: It was obvious from the start that you were a gifted child.
(Cue photo of Lily smothered in chocolate/pulling the cat's tail.)
And your very first achievement came early on, when you were awarded a prize for your cutting-edge artwork at nursery school, clearly leaning towards the *avant-garde*.
(Photo of three-year-old Lily holding painting.)
It was at about that time that you first came into contact with your oldest friend.

Birthday Surprises

Jess: Yes, Lily, and it took me ages to get that piece of Lego out of my left nostril!
(Jess enters from behind screen amid scenes of weeping, great joy, etc.)

. . . you get the idea. Include as many props as you can – these could be swimming certificates, school reports, items of clothing, etc. It's a lot of work, but your friend will definitely love this birthday surprise.

A Posh Surprise
David Beckham missed his wife's thirty-first birthday but made up for it with a surprise birthday treat: they flew to Paris in a jet filled with rose petals.

Chapter 3
PERFECT PRESENTS, CARDS AND CAKES

Are you stuck for ideas for someone special's birthday present? Of course, you could always nip out and buy them diamonds, a holiday in the Caribbean or a new designer wardrobe . . . unless you're not Bill Gates, in which case you'll need some inspiration.

> Jennifer Lopez bought a £2.5 million diamond-encrusted ring for a birthday present . . . to herself!

Perfect Presents

The best birthday gifts show that the giver has put some thought and effort into choosing them, and they don't have to be expensive. Before you hit the shops, it's a good idea to have a think about the person you're buying for so that you can give something that suits them. For example, what are their hobbies? What's their sense of humour like? Are they an indoor or an outdoor person? Use your pal's personal profile to pick the perfect present.

> "Gifts, believe me, captivate both men and gods."
> — Ovid, an Ancient Roman

A Gorgeous Gift List

Here are some ideas for presents that are sure to go down well when they're matched to the right person. If you're strapped for cash you can still give a great gift – some presents cost more time and energy than money, and often they're appreciated far more than expensive ones. Presents marked * are budget options (in fact, some are almost free).

Special Selection

Make up a Birthday Box containing lots of little things – favourite sweets, a key-ring, funky pens and pencils, lip balm, lipstick or other make-up items, small bottles of bubble bath or shampoo, costume jewellery . . . If there's room, place the month's birthday flower on the top. Use scrunched-up tissue paper inside to make it look lovely. If ready-made gift boxes are too expensive, you might find that a Birthday Bag is cheaper (or make your own).

Birthday Feast

Invite the birthday boy or girl to dinner or lunch (to be cooked by you). Draw up the invitation on a piece of card and make it look posh and professional.

**Nessie Leicester is invited to a Special Celebratory Dinner
(to be made by Mo "Cordon Bleu" Jones,
Chef Extraordinaire)
in honour of Nessie's Birthday
on 22 March at 6 p.m.
at 23 New Road.
Bring: nothing but your sparkling wit,
dazzling presence, etc.
RSVP**

You could invite some other friends, too, if you think it's a good idea and you're up to it. Or the invitation could be for a meal out, if you're feeling rich. Make sure it's for a day when you know your friend is free, and not too far from the birthday.

Movie Magic

Invite your birthday boy or girl to the movies. This could be rented DVDs at your place (you have to provide the popcorn, DVDs, etc), or a trip to the cinema – on you, of course. Or you could look out for other movie-related presents, like posters, star autographs, memorabilia . . . or even a dressable Brad Pitt paper doll. (Have a look on the Internet for other silly movie-star items.)

Galactic Gift

As an unusual gift for someone who's into science, you could name a star after the birthday boy or girl. It's not cheap – from about £20 – but maybe you could club together with a friend. Look on the Internet for details.

*Musical Masterpiece

Make a CD. This could simply be a collection of songs that you think the birthday boy or girl will like. Or, with a bit more effort, you could include one track from each year of his or her life (this will take a bit of research but the reaction will be worth it). It's a particularly good idea for a special birthday like a sixteenth, or oldsters' decade birthdays. If it's for someone young and you end up with a short CD, you might want to mix in some other tracks with a birthday theme (see below for ideas), or even include two songs per year. On the other hand, if it's for your dad's fortieth birthday you'll end up needing more than one CD and a lot of time for research. Make sure you include a well-designed playlist and cover: you could use your own artwork if you're good at that sort of thing, or use a photo or an image from a card or magazine for the cover; or, better still, make a collage of cuttings from magazines and photos that's relevant to your friend or relative (maybe put a cut-out photo of the birthday boy/girl as a baby in the centre of the CD cover).

> **Birthday Songs**
> *Birthday* by the Beatles
> *Happy Birthday* by Stevie Wonder
> *Lisa, It's Your Birthday* by Bart Simpson and Michael Jackson
> *Birthday* by Destiny's Child
> *Happy Birthday* by Altered Images
> *Happy Birthday* by New Kids on the Block

Go Wild

As an unusual birthday present for an animal lover, adopt an animal. There's a variety up for adoption – tigers, orcas, wolves, donkeys, otters, just about anything you can think of – from about £20. Adopting an animal means that you are helping to protect and care for endangered wildlife or an individual animal (without having to clear up after it!). Have a look at wwf.org or bornfree.org.

*Photo Fun

Find a flattering or funny photo of your friend or relative (note: it absolutely must be one you *know* they'll like – people can be very touchy about photos). There are plenty of cool-looking yet inexpensive frames about, or you could make a frame from papier mâché or decorated card. Even better, if you have enough photos you can make a photo montage – include some photos of friends, relatives, pets and special places as well as ones of the birthday girl or boy. If you can't find a decent frame that's big enough (or that suits your budget), you could use a simple clip frame for this.

Golden Goal
Buy a share in a football club for a football fan's birthday. Not all clubs offer shares, but it's worth asking your birthday boy or girl's team (or looking on the Internet). Shares are available from about £20.

> "There are three hundred and sixty-four days when you might get unbirthday presents ... and only one for birthday presents."
> Lewis Carroll, Through the Looking-Glass

Instant Birthday
If your friend's giving a birthday party, make up a Birthday Party Kit – include lots of streamers, party poppers, balloons, a Happy Birthday banner, birthday candles, indoor sparklers ... no one can have too much of this kind of stuff! You could also include some "instructions" for birthday parties (see page 9 for ideas). Put everything in a bag or box and wrap it beautifully.

*On This Day In History
Do some research about the day and year your friend or relative was born, and draw up a special birthday document: list famous people born on their birthday, world events that happened that day (use Chapter 4 of this book as a starting point), movies released and books published that year. Add some astrological and Chinese horoscope information. You could even make a mock-up newspaper for your friend or relative's birthday using your desktop publishing skills. You can buy old editions of newspapers for any given day and year – look on the Internet – but you'll find that these are expensive.

Present Promises
Give your friend an IOU for one choccie bar, magazine or other small treat every week for the next six months. It's the gift that keeps on giving . . .

> ### A Birthday Present Superstition
> If a friend gives you a knife as a present, an old superstition says that the friendship will end unless you give them a coin in return. Remember that the next time you rush out to buy a bread knife for your best mate.

*Tasty Treats
Make some cakes or biscuits and ice them with the birthday boy or girl's initials, or age, or a combination of both. You could cheat and buy some appetising cakes or biscuits and just do the icing part (you can buy disposable icing kits cheaply in supermarkets). Of course, icing takes skill, so be prepared to have to eat your mistakes.

Green Gifts
If your birthday boy or girl is keen to be green, perhaps you could buy them an acre of rainforest and help protect the environment. It costs about £25, so you might want to get together with another friend for this. You can also dedicate or plant a tree for about £20.

Themed Thoughts
Gift boxes are expensive; it's cheaper *and* more personal if you make up your own. Here are some ideas: a star sign gift box (including a mug/key-ring/T-shirt/anything you can find bearing your friend or relative's sign, plus a special reading); a chocoholic's

gift box; a bath-time or aromatherapy gift box; a candle gift box (include different kinds of candle, small candle holders and tea-lights). Decorate or wrap the box to make it look extra special and use scrunched-up tissue paper inside. Tie ribbons around some of the individual items if you like.

> "We make a living by what we get, we make a life by what we give."
> Winston Churchill

Adrenaline Rush

You could buy an adventurous friend or relative an amazing experience – scuba diving, a balloon ride, a flying lesson or a bungee jump. Most of these are expensive, but it might be possible to buy your pal the experience of a lifetime if there's a big group of you to chip in.

Or you could try making something a bit out of the ordinary that'll go with a bang . . .

Birthday Cracker

This is just like a Christmas cracker, except for a birthday. Well, why not?

WHAT YOU NEED:
The cardboard tube inside a loo roll (You could use a bigger cardboard tube, but you might not be able to find a cracker snapper to fit it, in which case you'll have to shout "bang" instead . . . which might be a bit embarrassing.)
Wrapping paper (or any kind of fairly thick

paper – you could decorate it yourself)
String, thread or ribbon (depending on how posh you want to be)
Scissors
Glue or sticky tape
A cracker snapper (look for them in craft shops)
Things to go in the crackers (there's not room for much so choose wisely), such as:
- a paper party hat (you can make this yourself – add a label or a badge saying *Birthday Girl/Boy*)
- sample-sized sachets of shampoo, moisturiser, bubble bath, etc
- small but cute pens, pencils or erasers
- hair bands
- wrapped sweets (If you're including chocolates, remember not to leave the finished cracker anywhere warm)
- a balloon
- lip balm or other small make-up items
- jewellery – maybe using the month's birthstone
- glitter or confetti so there's a shower when you pull the cracker

WHAT YOU DO:
- Cut out a piece of wrapping paper big enough to go around the tube (or whatever you're using) and overlap each end by about 10 cm.
- Put the cracker snapper (if you're using one) in the centre of the wrapping paper, then wrap the paper around the tube lengthways and glue or tape the join.

- Twist one end of the paper and tie with string, thread or ribbon.
- Put your goodies inside, and then twist the other end of the paper and tie that up, too.
- Pull the cracker with the birthday girl or boy and make sure they win!

Naked Surprise

Lady Caroline Lamb was married to the British Prime Minister Lord Melbourne and gave her husband a surprise on his birthday: she leaped naked from a large tureen served to him at his birthday banquet!

Wrap Up

Don't forget to wrap your presents beautifully. Here are some top tips.

- Cut simple shapes (stars, hearts, circles, flowers) out of coloured or shiny card to use as gift tags – make a hole for string or ribbon with a hole punch. Or you could cut out images from old cards or postcards to use as gift tags.
- Use ordinary brown paper as wrapping. Decorate it with spirals or squiggles in gold or silver pen. Or write the person's name, or *Happy Birthday* in different languages (see page 80).
- Finish the gift with ribbon, string or raffia (which looks especially classy with plain brown paper) tied in a bow.
- Make spirals by running a straight edge (e.g. a ruler) quickly along one side of wrapping ribbon.
- Glue spots or star shapes on plain wrapping and sprinkle glitter over it.
- Glue wrapped sweets onto the finished gift.

- Experiment with different colour combinations for your ribbon and wrapping (simple often works best). You could use your friend's favourite colour.
- Cut out an image (or images) from a magazine to stick on plain wrapping (it could be of your friend's favourite celebrity, for example). Or use a photo.
- Use a ready-made gift box or bag and add your own gift tag, ribbon spirals and bows.
- Make a paper flower or two to stick on your wrapped gift (see page 29).

Say "Happy Birthday" in . . .

French: Joyeux anniversaire
Finnish: Hyvaa syntymapaivaa
Arabic: Eed melad said
Spanish: Feliz cumpleaños
Danish: Tillykke med fodselsdagen
Hawaiian: Hau oli la hanau
Czech: Vsechno nejlepsi k tvym narozeniman
Dutch: Hartelikj gefeliciteerd metje verjaardag
Gaelic: Co latha breith sona dhut
Hindi: Janam din ki badhai
Icelandic: Til Hamingju med Afmaelisdaginn
Latin: Fortuna Dies Natalis
Gujarati: Janma divas mubarak
Vietnamese: Chuc mung sinh nhat
Polish: Wszystkiego najlepszego
Welsh: Penblwydd hapus

Birthday Cards

Bought cards can be funny, appropriate or pretty, but none of them will be quite as funny or appropriate as one you've made yourself (it might not be all that pretty, but that's not the main thing). A home-made card will be appreciated far more than a bought one and, of course, it shows you've put effort and thought into it. Along with your fabulously thoughtful and wonderful present, perhaps presented on a special birthday breakfast tray, a birthday card is an important part of your friend or relative's day – and they make easy-to-keep souvenirs.

Below are some different card-making ideas. The cards are all easy to make and don't need difficult-to-find components or complicated techniques. You can also buy card-making sets in most craft shops.

Collage Cards

WHAT YOU NEED:
Some fairly stiff card
PVA glue
Photos and/or cuttings from magazines – see below

WHAT YOU DO:
Get hold of a photo of your friend or family member and use that as the basis for the birthday card design. You could make a collage with cuttings from magazines and photos of things your friend likes: hobbies, movies, TV programmes, etc. Simply stick them on to your folded card with glue. You could use cut-out letters from magazines to spell *Happy Birthday*. Here are a few collage ideas.

- Stick your friend's head on to his or her favourite celebrity's body. Or, even better, stick the photo of your friend's head on to the body of someone in a passionate clinch with their favourite celebrity. Even if you don't get this perfect, it is bound to raise a laugh and be appreciated.
- Find a photo of your friend as a baby, and make up a collage with photos of other family members, favourite things, or just flowers cut from cards or magazines, or stars cut from shiny paper.
- Find photos of the birthday boy or girl as a baby, a toddler, aged five and aged eight or so – your friend through the ages. (It's probably going to be quite easy for you to do this if it's for a brother or sister, but it might be tricky getting hold of photos for a friend.)

A Pop-up Collage Card

If you can find a really good picture of your friend – preferably doing something funny such as jumping, punching the air, running, or just looking a bit wild-eyed – this is a great card to make. (The pop-up could also be of your friend's favourite celebrity – or indeed anything you like.) You can decorate the front of the card using one of the other ideas in this chapter: it could be a collage picture but doesn't have to be. It's all about the startling surprise inside . . .

WHAT YOU NEED
Stiff card
PVA glue
A cut-out photo or other image to pop up! You need

to make sure this image is at least 2 cm shorter than the width of the card, and make sure the paper's not so flimsy that it'll flop over (if it is, back it with stiffer paper or card).

WHAT YOU DO:
- Fold your card in half.
- Make four cuts as shown, each about 1.5 cm long, with the middle point between them being the centre of the card. (You'll need to work out exactly how far apart they need to be and how thick they need to be, depending on your image.)
- Open up the card, glue the bits of the tabs marked A and glue your image to them. Leave it to dry completely without shutting the card.
- When your friend opens the card, there will be a pop-up surprise to remember!

Stuck-on Cards

You can attach whatever you think looks good to the front of a plain home-made card – decorate the background first with some hand-drawn spirals, stars or swirls in gold or silver pen, or some little stickers. Then keep an eye out for fun things to attach to the front – you can pin or glue them on. This could be . . .

- a badge (advertising a favourite band, a political slogan, or just saying *Birthday Girl*, *5 Today* or similar)
- a wrapped sweet or lollipop (be careful it's not too heavy for the card you're using)
- a fridge magnet (though again you'll need to have heavy card for this)
- a key-ring
- earrings – leave them on their backing card and glue that to your birthday card
- stickers
- sequins, fake gemstones (you can get these in all shapes and sizes from craft shops – they're very cheap), beads, ribbon . . .

Simple Yet Classy Cards

Leaf Card

WHAT YOU NEED:
White or coloured card
Leaves – fern leaves look good
Spray paint
PVA glue
Glitter

What you do:
- Put down some newspaper or scrap paper to avoid spray-painting the furniture.
- Fold your card in half, open it again and cover one half of it (the back half of the finished card) with a piece of scrap paper, so it doesn't get sprayed.
- Put some leaves on the front of the card in an artistic arrangement – remember that less is more!
- Spray with paint (any colour you like – make sure it's a good contrast with the colour of the card; if your card is coloured, white paint can look good). Leave it to dry completely, then remove the leaves.
- Carefully dab some glue onto the edges of the leaf outlines (in an artistic manner), then shake over some glitter.
- Leave it to dry – et voilà.

Star Card

Use coloured card, and simply stick on a star made from felt, shiny card, corrugated card, or whatever you like. Decorate it with sequins or glitter.

Ribbon Card

Draw two or three parallel horizontal lines across the front of your card in pencil. Glue along the lines and stick ribbon to it. In between your ribbon stripes you could put sequins, fake gemstones or star stickers, or draw spirals or stars in gold or silver pen.

Brilliant Birthday Cakes

If you like cooking, or if you just really want to spoil someone, try one of these simple birthday cakes for someone special's birthday. It's a good idea to try out the recipe on your family first — that way you'll be sure it tastes lovely and you'll have some practice. But try not to eat it all yourself.

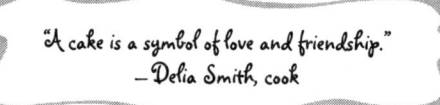

> "A cake is a symbol of love and friendship."
> — Delia Smith, cook

Cake-making Tips

- Always use the size of tin mentioned in the recipe. (If you use one that's too big, you'll end up with a pancake; use one that's too small, and it might spill over the top or have a dip in the middle.) Tins with push-out bottoms are easiest to use.
- Remember to pre-heat the oven.
- Don't open the oven door until at least three-quarters of the cooking time is up. (Try to avoid opening it during cooking if at all possible.)
- Ovens vary and you'll just have to get to know the one you use, there's no way around it. This is why it's a good idea to have a practice run at cakes, to avoid flat sponges and burnt offerings.
- To check if the cakes are cooked, see if they are beginning to come away from the sides of the tins. You can always insert a skewer in the middle, too; if the cake is ready, the skewer should come out clean.

Decadent Chocolate Cake

WHAT YOU NEED

For the cake:
2 20-cm round shallow cake tins, greased and the bases lined with baking paper
125 g butter, softened
225 g dark, soft brown sugar
2 medium-sized eggs
142 ml sour cream
175 g plain flour
1 tsp baking powder
1/2 tsp bicarbonate of soda
50 g cocoa

For the filling:
4 tbsp cocoa
250 g butter
300 g icing sugar, sieved
Vanilla essence

WHAT YOU DO
- Pre-heat the oven to 190°C/Gas Mark 5.
- To make the cake, mix the butter and sugar together (with an electric whisk or metal spoon). Keep going until the mixture is light and fluffy.
- Beat in the eggs a little at a time, and then add the sour cream and mix in. Don't worry if the mixture looks curdled at this stage.
- In a separate bowl, sieve together the plain flour, baking powder, bicarbonate of soda and cocoa, then gently tip this mix on top of the wet

mixture. Slowly fold in the dry ingredients ("folding" means stirring in very gently with a metal spoon, so that you lose as little air as possible) until all the ingredients are well mixed.

- Divide the mixture equally between the tins and bake for 30 – 35 minutes, until the cake is coming away from the sides of the tins slightly.
- Turn out the cakes on to a wire tray to cool.
- While the cake is cooling, you can make the filling. Mix the cocoa with 4 tbsp of boiling water to make a smooth paste, then allow this to cool.
- In the meantime, mix the butter with the sieved icing sugar and 5 drops of vanilla essence until light and fluffy, then add in the cocoa paste and mix well.
- When the cake is cool, put half the filling on top of one half, put the other layer of sponge on top, then smother the top and sides of the cake with the rest of the filling mix.
- Decorate the top with nuts or grated white chocolate.

A Birthday Superstition

If you blow out all your birthday candles with one breath and make a wish, your wish will come true.

Fruit Birthday Cake

What You Need:
20-cm round cake tin, greased and the base lined with baking paper
120 g margarine
170 g sugar
340 g dried fruit
225 ml water
1 tsp bicarbonate of soda
1/2 tsp of mixed spice
2 large eggs, beaten
120 g plain flour
120 g self-raising flour

What You Do:
- Pre-heat the oven to 180°C/Gas Mark 4.
- Put the margarine, sugar, fruit, water, bicarbonate of soda and mixed spice into a saucepan and heat it gently. Bring it to the boil and let it simmer for one minute.
- Pour the mixture into a bowl and let it cool – it's important that you do this, otherwise when you add the eggs they'll start to cook too soon.
- Add the eggs, flour and salt. Mix everything really well and pour it into the cake tin.
- Bake for about 1 1/4 hours. Check it at about 50 minutes – if the cake looks dark brown on top, cover it with silver foil.
- Allow the cake to cool completely before adding the icing of your choice (see page 93 – 97 for different types of icing and other decorations).

Birthday Sponge Cake

What You Need:

For the cake:

2 20-cm round cake tins, 4 cm deep, greased and the base lined with baking paper, greaseproof paper or parchment

175 g self-raising flour
1 rounded tsp baking powder
3 large eggs
175 g soft butter
175 g caster sugar
1/2 tsp of vanilla extract

For the filling:

Use a layer of your favourite jam and a layer of whipped cream, or just the jam, or some summer fruits (raspberries, strawberries, etc) mashed up with some sugar to your taste.

What You Do:

- Pre-heat the oven to 170°C/Gas Mark 3.
- Sift the flour and baking powder into a large bowl.
- Add all the other cake ingredients and whisk everything together (use an electric whisk if you have one, or a wooden spoon and plenty of elbow grease). It's ready when a spoonful of the mixture will drop off the spoon fairly easily.
- Divide the mixture evenly between the two cake tins, level them out with the back of a spoon and bake for 20–25 minutes. *Don't* be tempted to open the oven door and look before twenty minutes, or they'll be very

Brilliant Birthday Cakes

sad-looking sponge cakes.
- When you've taken the cakes out of the oven, wait for 5 – 10 minutes and then turn them out on to a cooling rack. When they're completely cold, put the first sponge on a plate or cake stand, spread your filling over it and put the other sponge on top.
- Ice the cake with one of the easy icings on page 93. (Or you could just dust the top with icing sugar.)

Birthday Pie
Instead of a birthday cake, many Russian children are given a birthday pie, with a message carved into the pie crust.

Individual Birthday Cakes

Even if you don't like cooking, you could try making some fairy cakes. They are very easy (you just have to remember to pre-heat the oven, and to take them out before they burn). Use the recipe for sponge cake on page 90 and cook at 200°C/Gas Mark 6 for 15 – 20 minutes, or use a packet mix if you want to be really lazy. Put a blob of icing and a birthday candle in the middle of each cake – with the lights dimmed, a tray full of little candles will look gorgeous. Or you could use sweets, glacé cherries, etc instead of candles. Depending on how many people there are, the birthday girl or boy might need some help in blowing out all the candles. But don't worry, their wish will still come true.

Carrot Cake

What You Need:

20-cm round cake tin, greased and the base lined with baking paper

225 g butter

225 g light brown sugar

4 large eggs, separated (this means separate the yolk from the white – the easiest way is to put an eggcup over the yolk and then tip the white into a bowl)

Grated rind of half an orange

1 tbsp lemon juice

175 g self-raising flour

1 tsp baking powder

50 g ground almonds

125 g chopped walnuts

350 g peeled and grated carrots

What You Do:

- Pre-heat the oven to 180 ºC/Gas Mark 4.
- Mix the butter and sugar together in a bowl until the mixture's pale and fluffy.
- Beat in the egg yolks, and then the orange rind and lemon juice.
- Sift the flour and baking powder and fold them into the mixture, and then fold in the ground almonds and walnuts ("folding" means stirring in very gently with a metal spoon, so that you lose as little air as possible).
- Whisk the egg whites until they're stiff (this is good exercise) and then fold them into the cake mixture with the grated carrots.

Brilliant Birthday Cakes

- Pour the mixture into the cake tin and bake for 75–90 minutes. (Check at just over an hour – if the top's looking dark brown, put some silver foil over it.)
- When you take the cake out of the oven, leave it for about 10 minutes, and then turn it out onto a wire rack to cool.
- Once the cake is cool (and not before), add the topping of your choice.

> "I don't even butter my bread; I consider that cooking."
> — Katherine Cebrian

The Icing on the Cake

Fondant Icing

The easiest icing of all is the kind you buy ready-made in supermarkets. You'll find fondant icing in 225 g packs – use three packs to ice a cake made in a 20-cm cake tin. Simply dust the work surface with icing sugar and roll out the icing with a rolling pin so that it's a big enough circle to completely cover the cake and sides. Carefully lift it onto the cake, smooth down the sides and trim off the excess icing.

Simple Icing

What You Need:
250 g icing sugar
3 tbsp water
Food colouring (if you like)

What You Do:
Sift the icing sugar into a bowl and gradually mix in the water, along with the food colouring if you're using it.

Buttercream Icing

You can buy ready-made buttercream icing in supermarkets, but it's easy to make.

What You Need:
125 g soft butter
225 g sifted icing sugar
2 – 4 drops vanilla essence
1 – 2 tbsp milk

What You Do:
- Cream the butter with a fork until it's really soft.
- Gradually add the icing sugar, vanilla essence and milk, beating it all the time.
- To make coffee buttercream, leave out the vanilla essence and milk and add 2 tsp of instant coffee dissolved in 1–2 tbsp of hot water, but make sure this cools before you add it to the butter and icing sugar. To make chocolate buttercream, leave out 2 tsp of icing sugar and replace with 2 tsp of cocoa.

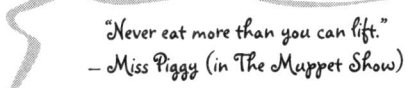

> "Never eat more than you can lift."
> – Miss Piggy (in The Muppet Show)

Chocolate Icing

WHAT YOU NEED:
150 ml double cream
125 g good-quality plain chocolate, broken into pieces

WHAT YOU DO:
- Put the cream in a small saucepan and bring it to the boil.
- Off the heat, add the chocolate and stir it gently until the chocolate has melted and the mixture is smooth.
- Return it to the heat and bring it back to the boil.
- Take it off the heat again and let it cool down to room temperature before icing your cake. It'll be the same texture as softened butter (but it'll taste a lot nicer).

Creamy Icing

WHAT YOU NEED:
250 g mascarpone (soft cheese)
200 ml fromage frais
1 dessertspoon of caster sugar

WHAT YOU DO:
- Simply mix everything together and spread it over your cake. You could add some chopped nuts or food colouring if you wish.

Carrot Cake Icing

(You can use this for other kinds of cake too.)

WHAT YOU NEED:
225g full fat soft cheese (any kind)
2 tsp runny honey
1 tsp lemon juice

WHAT YOU DO:
- Simply mix everything together and spread it over your cake. Add some food colouring if you like, or scatter some chopped walnuts on the top.

A Bit of a Bash
There was a huge party to celebrate the eighty-ninth birthday of Colonel Sanders, the founder of Kentucky Fried Chicken. It was the biggest birthday party ever, with 35,000 guests.

Candles

The tradition is to put one candle on the birthday cake for every year of the person's life. But if you're making a cake for your mum, let's face it: you're not going to be able to fit that many candles on the top. An alternative is to put a single candle in the middle (decorate the cake with other things as well – see below), or spell her name with candles. You can find candles that are impossible to blow out, if you want to see the birthday girl or boy going blue in the face.

Sweets

Sweets can look lovely dotted about on top of a birthday cake (and of course they taste good, too). Try Smarties or M&Ms, or Maltesers for a chocolate cake. But any small sweets can work well – jelly babies, chocolate mice, cola cubes . . .

Marzipan

Colour marzipan with food colouring and cut out shapes to stick on top of your cake. Or you could dot the cake with coloured marzipan balls.

Fruit

Pile strawberries, raspberries and blueberries on top of a cake iced with fondant icing, and sprinkle them with a little icing sugar if you like.

In fact, there are hundreds of things you can use to decorate your cake: nuts (halved walnuts look good), glacé cherries, flowers (but make sure you don't use anything poisonous!), piped icing (this will take practice), ready-made sugar flowers, hundreds and thousands, edible glitter sprinkles . . .

Chapter 4
BIRTHDAYS THROUGH THE YEAR

So you're raring to go; you want to organise that party, make some scrumptious food, design a dazzling card and give the most thoughtful present. But just maybe you need a little help to get an idea to set you off or to make things that little bit more special for the birthday boy or girl.

Well, this chapter not only lists some interesting things that have happened on every birthday, but also shows who else was born on that day. So whenever you were born, you can find out what makes that date special (apart from the fact it's your birthday, of course). Maybe you share a birthday with Orlando Bloom, Queen Victoria or Madonna. Or maybe your birthday's the anniversary of the first moon landing or the first-ever episode of *EastEnders*.

The chapter also contains information about the months of the year, and details of all the star signs. Use it as a reference section, and you'll soon have loads of ideas and fascinating facts to put into your planning.

January

January was named after the ancient Roman god, Janus, the god of doorways, who had two faces, one looking forwards and one looking backwards. The Saxons named the month of January Wulf-monath, or wolf month.

Birthstone: Garnet
Flower: Carnation or snowdrop
Star Signs: Capricorn (see page 167) and . . .

Aquarius
(the Water Carrier)
Dates: 21 January – 19 February
Ruling Planet: Uranus
Element: Air

Does this sound anything like you? If you're an Aquarian, you're supposed to be intelligent, independent, logical and strong-willed. People might accuse you of being aloof and detached, though.

January Birthdays

1 JANUARY

1 January is New Year's Day. On 1 January 1660, Samuel Pepys made the first entry in his famous diary. And on 1 January 1964, Top of the Pops was first broadcast.
You share a birthday with:
E M Forster, writer of Howards End (1879), J Edgar Hoover, founder of the modern FBI (1895), J D Salinger, writer of The Catcher in the Rye (1919).

2 JANUARY

On 2 January 1968, Dr Christiaan Bernard performed the first heart transplant.
You share a birthday with:
Isaac Asimov, science-fiction writer (1920), Cuba Gooding Jr, actor (1968).

3 JANUARY

On 3 January 1924, English explorer Howard Carter discovered the tomb of Tutankhamun in Egypt.
You share a birthday with:
Cicero, Roman philosopher (106 BC), J R R Tolkien, writer of Lord of the Rings (1892), Mel Gibson, actor (1956).

4 JANUARY

On 4 January 1958, Sir Edmund Hillary arrived at the South Pole. On 4 January 2000, the first women reached the South Pole.
You share a birthday with:
Jacob Grimm, fairytale writer (1785), Louis Braille, creator of reading and writing system for the blind (1809).

5 JANUARY

On 5 January 1896, German physicist Wilhelm Roentgen discovered X-rays.
You share a birthday with:
Umberto Eco, writer (1929), Diane Keaton, actress (1946), Marilyn Manson, singer (1969).

6 JANUARY

On January 6 1066, Harold II was crowned King of England (but he soon lost the crown to William the Conqueror). 6 January is also Twelfth Night – it's supposed to be bad luck if you don't take your Christmas decorations down by the end of today.
You share a birthday with:
Saint Joan of Arc (1412), Rowan Atkinson, actor and comedian (1955), Anthony Minghella, film director (1956).

7 JANUARY

On 7 January 1785, Frenchman Jean-Pierre Blanchard and American John Jeffries became the first people to cross the Channel by air when they flew from Dover to Calais in a gas balloon. 7 January is also Christmas Day in the Russian Orthodox Church.
You share a birthday with:
Saint Bernadette of Lourdes (1844), Gerald Durrell, naturalist and writer (1925), Nicholas Cage, actor (1964).

8 JANUARY

On 8 January 794, Viking invaders attacked Lindisfarne Island in the earliest recorded Viking raid. And Italian astronomer Galileo Galilei died on 8 January 1642, aged 77.
You share a birthday with:
Elvis Presley, singer (1935), Stephen Hawking, physicist (1942), David Bowie, singer (1947).

Norwegian Birthdays
If it's your birthday in Norway, the tradition is for you and a friend to perform a song and dance in front of your class at school.

9 JANUARY
On 9 January 1768, Englishman Philip Astley staged the first modern circus in London. And on 9 January 1806, Lord Horatio Nelson was buried in Saint Paul's Cathedral.
You share a birthday with:
Richard Nixon, former US President (1913), Joely Richardson, actress (1965).

10 JANUARY
On 10 January 1863, London's underground railway was opened.
You share a birthday with:
Gregory Rasputin, the 'mad monk' who was advisor to Tsar Nicholas II of Russia (1869), Rod Stewart, singer (1945), George Foreman, boxer (1949).

11 JANUARY
On 11 January 1569, the first recorded lottery took place in England. And on 11 January 1928, Leon Trotsky, one of the leaders of the Russian Revolution, was banished to a remote part of the Soviet Union by Soviet leader Joseph Stalin.
You share a birthday with:
Mary J Blige, singer (1971), Emile Heskey, footballer (1978).

12 JANUARY
On 12 January 1932, Ophelia Wyatt Caraway became the first woman to be elected to the United States Senate.
You share a birthday with:
Charles Perrault, author of fairy tales such as *Cinderella* and *Sleeping Beauty* (1628), Jack London, writer (1876).

13 JANUARY
On 13 January 1930, the Mickey Mouse comic strip first appeared.
You share a birthday with:
Stephen Hendry, snooker champion (1969), Orlando Bloom, actor (1977).

14 JANUARY
On 14 January 1690, the clarinet was invented. In 1990, *The Simpsons* premiered on Fox-TV.
You share a birthday with:
Hugh Lofting, author and illustrator of *Dr Dolittle* (1886), Faye Dunaway, actress (1941), LL Cool J, singer (1968).

15 JANUARY
On 15 January 1559, Elizabeth I was crowned Queen of England.
You share a birthday with:
Martin Luther King Junior, preacher and civil rights campaigner (1929), Aristotle Onassis, Greek billionaire (1906).

16 JANUARY
On 16 January 1759, the British Museum opened in London. And on 16 January 1919, Prohibition (the banning of alcohol) began in the USA.
You share a birthday with:
Kate Moss, model (1974), Aaliyah, singer and actress (1979).

17 JANUARY
On 17 January 1950, an armoured car depot in Boston, USA, was robbed of $2 million – the event became famous as the Great Brinks Robbery.
You share a birthday with:
Al Capone, gangster (1899), Muhammad Ali (born Cassius Clay), boxer (1942), Jim Carrey, actor and comedian (1962).

18 JANUARY
On 18 January 1912, Captain Robert Falcon Scott reached the South Pole, only to find that Roald Amundsen, the Norwegian explorer, had got there first.
You share a birthday with:
A A Milne, writer of *Winnie the Pooh* (1882), Oliver Hardy, actor and comedian (1892), Kevin Costner, actor and film director (1955).

19 JANUARY
On 19 January 1966, Indira Gandhi became India's first female prime minister.
You share a birthday with:
James Watt, inventor (1736), Edgar Allan Poe, horror writer (1809), Paul Cezanne, artist (1939), Dolly Parton, country singer (1946).

20 JANUARY
On January 20 1961, John F Kennedy became the thirty-fifth President of the USA.
You share a birthday with:
Buzz Aldrin, astronaut (1930), Gary Barlow, singer (1971).

> **A January Superstition**
> If you want to find out who you're going to marry: on the Eve of St Agnes (the night before 21 January) stick a pin in the sleeve of your nightie. You'll dream of the person you'll marry.

21 JANUARY
On January 21 1976, two of the world's first supersonic aircraft, Concorde, took off from London and Paris at the same time with their first passengers.
You share a birthday with:
Christian Dior, designer (1905), Geena Davis, actress (1957), Emma Bunton, singer with the Spice Girls (1976).

22 JANUARY
On 22 January 1901, Queen Victoria died and her son, Edward VII, became King of the United Kingdom.
You share a birthday with:
Lord Byron, poet (1788), George Balanchine, composer and choreographer (1904).

23 JANUARY
23 January 638 was the start of the Islamic calendar.
You share a birthday with:
Edouard Manet, Impressionist artist (1832), Princess Caroline of Monaco (1957).

24 JANUARY
On 24 January 41 AD, evil Roman Emperor Caligula was assasinated. On 24 January 1908, the Boy Scouts movement began in England.
You share a birthday with:
Edith Wharton, writer (1862), Nastassja Kinski, actress (1960), Mischa Barton, actress (1986).

25 JANUARY
25 January is Burns Night, when the Scottish poet Robert Burns is commemorated with poems and haggis.
You share a birthday with:
Robert Burns, poet (1759), Virginia Woolf, writer (1882), Alicia Keys, singer (1981).

26 JANUARY
On 26 January 1905, the world's largest diamond, known as the Cullinan, was discovered at a mine in Pretoria, South Africa. And on 26 January 1950, India became a republic and the most highly populated democracy in the world.
You share a birthday with:
Emperor Go-Nara of Japan (1497), King Charles XIV of Sweden (1763), Paul Newman, actor (1925), Eartha Kitt, singer (1928).

27 JANUARY
On 27 January 1926, John Logie Baird gave the first public demonstration of his television.

You share a birthday with:
Wolfgang Amadeus Mozart, composer (1756), Lewis Carroll, writer of *Alice's Adventures in Wonderland* (1832).

28 JANUARY
On 28 January 1547, nine-year-old Edward VI succeeded Henry VIII as King of England.
You share a birthday with:
Jackson Pollock, artist (1912), Elijah Wood, actor (1981).

29 JANUARY
On 29 January 1856, Queen Victoria issued the first Victoria Cross, to recognise acts of bravery during the Crimean War of 1854-55. On 29 January 1820, King George III died after suffering ten years of mental illness.
You share a birthday with:
Anton Chekhov, writer (1860), Oprah Winfrey, TV host (1954), Heather Graham, actress (1970).

30 JANUARY
After bitter civil war in England, King Charles I was beheaded at the hands of his own government on 30 January 1649.
You share a birthday with:
Franklin D Roosevelt, former US President (1882), Gene Hackman, actor (1930), Vanessa Redgrave, actress (1937), Phil Collins, singer (1951).

31 JANUARY
On 31 January 1971, *Apollo 14* was launched on a successful manned mission to the moon (the astronauts later played golf on the moon's surface).
You share a birthday with:
John Lydon (aka Johnny Rotten), singer (1956), Minnie Driver, actress (1971), Justin Timberlake, singer (1981).

Snowdrop

February

February was named by the ancient Romans after Februus, the god of purification. It was the last month of the ancient Roman calendar, but every so often an extra month had to be added in after February because the Roman months didn't quite tie in with the seasons. We do a similar thing when we add in an extra day at the end of February every four years – 29 February.

Birthstone: Amethyst
Flower: Violet
Star Signs: Aquarius (see page 101) and . . .

Pisces (the Fish)
Dates: 20 February – 20 March
Ruling Planet: Neptune
Element: Water

Does this sound anything like you? If you're born under the sign of Pisces, you're supposed to be kind, sensitive, creative and sympathetic. If that sounds too good to be true, the downside is that you might also be secretive and perhaps easily led.

February Birthdays

1 FEBRUARY
On 1 February 1587, Queen Elizabeth I signed the death warrant for her cousin, Mary Queen of Scots, leading to her execution.
You share a birthday with:
Muriel Spark, writer (1918), Boris Yeltsin, former President of Russia (1931), Lisa Marie Presley, daughter of Elvis (1968).

> **Pucker up!**
> If you kiss a passionfruit on 1 February your dreams are supposed to come true!

2 FEBRUARY
2 February is the Christian feast day of Candlemass, when candles are lit in special church services.
You share a birthday with:
Nell Gwyn, orange seller and girlfriend of King Charles II (1650), James Joyce, writer (1882), Shakira, singer (1977).

> **Snowdrop superstition**
> An old superstition says that if you bring snowdrops into the house before Candlemass Day, you will have bad luck.

3 FEBRUARY
On 3 February 1966, the unmanned Russian spacecraft *Lunik 9* landed on the moon, in the first ever controlled moon landing.
You share a birthday with:
Isla Fisher, actress (1976), Tallulah Belle Willis, third daughter of movie stars Bruce Willis and Demi Moore (1994).

4 FEBRUARY
On 4 February 1789, George Washington was elected the first president of the USA.
You share a birthday with:
Rosa Parks, American civil rights campaigner (1913), Natalie Imbruglia, singer (1975).

5 FEBRUARY
On 5 February 1953, children flocked to sweet shops as the sweet rationing which began during World War II had finally finished. On 5th February 1988, Comic Relief held its first Red Nose Day in the UK to raise money for charities.
You share a birthday with:
Robert Peel, former UK Prime Minister (1788), Bobby Brown, singer and husband of Whitney Houston (1969).

6 FEBRUARY
On 6 February 1952, King George VI died and Queen Elizabeth II succeeded to the throne.
You share a birthday with:
Queen Anne of the United Kingdom (1665), Ronald Reagan, actor and former US President (1911), Bob Marley, reggae singer (1945), Axl Rose, rock singer (1962).

7 FEBRUARY
On 7th February 1964, the Beatles were greeted by 25,000 fans when they arrived for the first time in the USA. And on 7 February 1971, women were granted the right to vote in Switzerland.
You share a birthday with:
Charles Dickens, writer (1812), Chris Rock, comedian and actor (1966), Ashton Kutcher, actor (1978).

February

8 February
On 8 February 1725, Emperor Peter the Great of Russia died. On 8 February 1587, Mary Queen of Scots was executed at Fotheringay Castle.
You share a birthday with:
Jules Verne, writer (1828), James Dean, actor (1931), John Grisham, writer (1955).

9 February
On 9 February 1960, the first-ever star on the Hollywood Walk of Fame was given to actress Joanne Woodward. And on 9 February 1971, *Apollo 14* safely returned to Earth after the third manned moon landing.
You share a birthday with:
Carmen Miranda, actress (1909), Alice Walker, writer (1944), Mena Suvari, actress (1979).

10 February
On 10 February 1840, Queen Victoria married Prince Albert. And on 10 February 1931, New Delhi became the capital of India.
You share a birthday with:
Mark Spitz, Olympic champion swimmer (1950), Laura Dern, actress (1967).

11 February
On 11 February 1975, Margaret Thatcher became the first female leader of the British Conservative Party. And on 11 February 1990, Nelson Mandela was freed from prison in South Africa, having been a political prisoner for 27 years.
You share a birthday with:
Thomas Alva Edison, inventor (1847), Sheryl Crow, singer (1963), Jennifer Aniston, actress (1969), Kelly Rowland, singer (1981).

12 February
On 12 February 1554, Lady Jane Grey was beheaded, after just nine days as the Queen of England.
You share a birthday with:
Charles Darwin, scientist (1809), Abraham Lincoln, former US President (1809), Judy Blume, writer (1938), "Prince" Naseem Hamed, boxer (1974), Christina Ricci, actress (1980).

13 February
On 13 February 1999, James Sunley of the United Kingdom recorded the fastest bobsled descent at the Cresta Run, St Moritz, Switzerland. He shot down the 1,212 metre-long ice run at an average speed of 87.11 km/hr (54.13 mph), taking just 50.09 seconds to complete the run.
You share a birthday with:
Jerry Springer, TV host (1944), Robbie Williams, singer (1974).

14 February
14 February is, of course, Valentine's Day. And on 14 February 1929, seven gangsters, rivals of Al Capone, were killed in a Chicago warehouse – this became famous as the Valentine's Day Massacre.
You share a birthday with:
Zahir-ud-din Mohammad Babur, Emperor of India and founder of the Moghul Dynasty, (1483), Kevin Keegan, footballer and manager (1951).

15 February
On 15 February 1971, the UK changed its money from pounds, shillings and pence to the decimal system we have today. And on 15 February 2003, between 10 and 15 million people in 600 cities worldwide protested against the war in Iraq, in the biggest day of protest in history.
You share a birthday with:
Galileo Galilei, scientist (1564), Matt Groening, creator of *The Simpsons* (1954).

16 February
On 16 February 1959, Fidel Castro became the prime minister of Cuba. In 2005, the Kyoto Protocol came into force. This was an agreement between 141 countries to curb

the air pollution blamed for global warming – however, the world's top polluter, the USA, did not sign up.
You share a birthday with:
Iain Banks, writer (1954), John McEnroe, tennis player (1959), Christopher Eccleston, actor and the ninth Doctor Who (1964).

> "Our birthdays are feathers in the broad wing of time."
> — Jean-Paul Richter, German author

17 FEBRUARY
On 17 February 1958, Pope Pius XII declared Saint Clare of Assisi the patron saint of television. On 17 Feburary 1924, the chimes of Big Ben were first used as a time signal by the BBC.
You share a birthday with:
King William III of the Netherlands (1817), Michael Jordan, US basketball player (1963), Paris Hilton, heiress and actress (1981).

18 FEBRUARY
On 18 February 1930, the planet Pluto, the ninth planet in our solar system and furthest away from the sun, was discovered.
You share a birthday with:
Mary Tudor, Queen of England (1516), Enzo Ferrari, racing-car driver and manufacturer (1898), John Travolta, actor (1954).

19 FEBRUARY
On 19 February 1986, the Soviet Union launched the Mir space station. And on 19 February 1985, the soap opera *EastEnders* was shown for the first time.
You share a birthday with:
Nicolas Copernicus, astronomer (1473), Prince Andrew of the United Kingdom (1960), Benicio Del Toro, actor (1967).

20 FEBRUARY
On 20 February 1472, the Orkney and Shetland Islands became part of Scotland. On 20 February 1962, spaceman John Glenn became the first American to orbit the Earth, landing safely in the Atlantic Ocean.
You share a birthday with:
Sidney Poitier, actor (1924), Mike Leigh, film director (1943), Cindy Crawford, model (1966).

21 FEBRUARY
On 21 February 1848, *The Communist Manifesto* by Karl Marx and Friedrich Engels was published in London.
You share a birthday with:
Tsar Peter III of Russia (1728), Nina Simone, singer (1933), Charlotte Church, singer (1986).

22 FEBRUARY
On 22 February 1997, scientists announced that they had successfully cloned a sheep called Dolly, the world's first cloned mammal.
You share a birthday with:
George Washington, first US president (1732), Julie Walters, actress (1950), Drew Barrymore, actress (1975).

23 FEBRUARY
On 23 February 1836, the Siege of the Alamo began in Texas. On 23 February 1660, Charles XI became King of Sweden. And on 23 February 1934, Leopold III became King of Belgium.
You share a birthday with:
Samuel Pepys, diarist (1633), Sylvie Guillem, ballerina (1965), Dakota Fanning, actress (1994).

24 FEBRUARY
On 24 February 1946, Juan Peron was elected President of Argentina. He and his

wife Eva (Evita) became immensely popular and he was re-elected twice. And on 24 February 1992, Nirvana singer Kurt Cobain married Courtney Love.
You share a birthday with:
Wilhelm Grimm, fairytale author (1786), Steven Jobs, computer pioneer (1955), Billy Zane, actor (1966).

25 FEBRUARY

On 25 February 1570, Queen Elizabeth I was excommunicated from the Catholic Church by the Pope, because of her persecution of Roman Catholics in England. On 25 February 1954, Gamal Abdul Nasser became President of Egypt.
You share a birthday with:
Pierre-Auguste Renoir, artist (1841), George Harrison, singer with the Beatles (1943), Tea Leoni, actress (1966).

26 FEBRUARY

On 26 February 364 AD, Valentinian I became Emperor of Rome. On 26 February 1949, an aircraft called the *Lucky Lady II* took off from Texas on the first non-stop flight around the world.
You share a birthday with:
Victor Hugo, writer (1802), Johnny Cash, singer (1932), Michael Bolton, singer (1953).

27 FEBRUARY

On 27 February 1900, the British Labour Party was founded. On 27 February 1964, the Italian government announced that it would accept suggestions on how to stop the leaning tower of Pisa leaning.
You share a birthday with:
John Steinbeck, writer (1902), Elizabeth Taylor, actress (1932), Chelsea Clinton, daughter of former US President Bill Clinton (1980).

28 FEBRUARY

On 28 February 1935, nylon was invented by Wallace Carothers.

You share a birthday with:
Linus Pauling, Nobel Prize-winning scientist (1901), Mario Andretti, racing driver (1940).

29 FEBRUARY

29 February occurs in a leap year (only once every four years). It is the traditional day for women to propose to men. On 29 February 1940, the film *Gone with the Wind* received 8 Oscars from the American Academy of Motion Picture Arts and Sciences.
You share a birthday with:
Jack Lousma, astronaut (1936), Ja Rule, rapper (1976).

Violet

March

March was originally the first month of the ancient Roman calendar, and was named after Mars, the Roman god of war. Mars was the father of the legendary founder of Rome, Romulus, and this gave the Ancient Romans an excuse to celebrate – the month of March was a non-stop party. In fact, it was so full of fun and celebrations that there was a special day set aside for everyone to have a rest!

Birthstone: Aquamarine or bloodstone
Flower: Daffodil
Star Signs: Pisces (see page 107) and . . .

Aries (the Ram)
Dates: 21 March – 20 April
Ruling Planet: Mars
Element: Fire

Does this sound anything like you? People born under the sign of Aries are supposed to be dynamic, vivacious characters who love a challenge and make good leaders. But they might also be a bit selfish and impatient.

March Birthdays

1 March

1 March is Saint David's Day – in Wales it's traditional to wear one of the Welsh emblems, a daffodil or a leek.
You share a birthday with:
Sandro Botticelli, painter (1445), Frédéric Chopin, composer (1810), Ron Howard, film director (1954).

2 March

On 2 March 1946, Ho Chi Minh became President of North Vietnam. And on 2 March 1972, the *Pioneer 10* spaceprobe was launched from Cape Canaveral, Florida, on a mission to Jupiter.
You share a birthday with:
Dr Seuss, writer of *The Cat in the Hat* (1904), Mikhail Gorbachev, former President of the USSR (1931), Chris Martin, singer (1977).

3 March

The opera *Carmen* premiered on 3 March 1875. And on 3 March 1955, Elvis Presley appeared on television for the first time.
You share a birthday with:
King John II of Portugal (1455), Alexander Graham Bell, inventor of the telephone (1847), Ronan Keating, singer (1977).

4 March

On 4 March 1861, Abraham Lincoln became the sixteenth US president. And on March 4 1933, Franklin D Roosevelt became the thirty-second president of United States.
You share a birthday with:
Antonio Vivaldi, composer (1678), Patsy Kensit, actress (1962).

Kissing Friday

Ash Wednesday usually falls in February or March. The Friday after it used to be known as Kissing Friday. The tradition was that schoolboys were allowed to kiss girls without being told to get lost. A Leicestershire tradition was that men could ask any woman they liked for a kiss, and if they were rejected, they were allowed to pinch the woman's bum! Thankfully, neither of these old traditions survives today.

---

5 March

On 5 March 1936, the Spitfire fighter aircraft made its maiden flight from Hampshire.
You share a birthday with:
Pier Paolo Pasolini, Italian film director (1922), Andy Gibb, singer with the Bee Gees (1958), Niki Taylor, model (1975).

6 March

On 6 March 1953, Georgi Malenkov became leader of the Communist Party of the Soviet Union, succeeding Joseph Stalin.
You share a birthday with:
Michelangelo Buonarotti, sculptor, painter and poet (1475), Elizabeth Barrett Browning, writer (1806), Shaquille O'Neal, basketball player (1972).

7 March

On 7 March 161 AD, Marcus Aurelius and Lucius Verus became co-Emperors of Rome.

And on 7 March 1912, Roald Amundsen announced that he had reached the South Pole (though he'd actually got there on 14 December 1911).
You share a birthday with:
Pope Clement XIII (1693), Viv Richards, cricketer (1952), Rachel Weisz, actress (1971).

8 MARCH
On 8 March 1702, Anne Stuart became Queen of England, Ireland and Scotland. 8 March is also International Women's Day.
You share a birthday with:
Kenneth Grahame, writer of *The Wind in the Willows* (1859), Lynn Redgrave, actress (1943), Freddie Prinze Jr, actor (1976).

9 MARCH
On 9 March 1796, Napoleon Bonaparte married Josephine de Beauharnais. And on 9 March 1959, the Barbie doll was seen for the first time at a toy fair in New York City.
You share a birthday with:
Yuri Gagarin, Soviet cosmonaut and the first man to travel into space (1934), Juliette Binoche, actress (1964).

10 MARCH
On 10 March 1876, inventor Alexander Graham Bell spoke to his assistant in another room over the telephone, saying, "Mr Watson, come here, I want you," – the first time speech was transmitted over a telephone system.
You share a birthday with:
Prince Edward of the United Kingdom (1964), Sharon Stone, actress (1958), Eva Herzigova, model (1973).

11 MARCH
On 11 March 1818, *Frankenstein* by Mary Wollstonecraft Shelley was published.
You share a birthday with:
Harold Wilson, former UK Prime Minister (1916), Douglas Adams, author of *The Hitchhiker's Guide to the Galaxy* (1952), Johnny Knoxville, actor (1971), Thora Birch, actress (1982).

12 MARCH
On 12 March 1923, inventor Lee de Forest demonstrated the first piece of film capable of recording sound.
You share a birthday with:
Vaslav Nijinsky, ballet dancer and choreographer (1890), Jack Kerouac, writer (1922), Liza Minnelli, singer and actress (1946).

13 MARCH
On 13 March 1781, William Hershel discovered the seventh planet from the sun, Uranus.
You share a birthday with:
Joseph Priestley, scientist and fizzy drinks inventor (1733), L Ron Hubbard, founder of the Church of Scientology (1911).

14 MARCH
In 1991, the "Birmingham Six" (six men found guilty of the IRA bombing of pubs in Birmingham in 1974) were set free after sixteen years of wrongful imprisonment.
You share a birthday with:
Albert Einstein, scientist (1879), Michael Caine, actor (1933), Billy Crystal, actor (1947).

15 MARCH
On 15 March 44 BC, Gaius Julius Caesar, dictator of Rome, was stabbed to death in the Senate house by sixty conspirators.
You share a birthday with:
Eduard Strauss, composer (1835), Eva Longoria, actress (1975).

Brazilian Birthdays

In Brazil, the birthday boy or girl gets a pull on the earlobe for each year of his or her life!

16 March

On 16 March 1521, Ferdinand Magellan became the first European to reach the Philippines.

You share a birthday with:
Emperor Ninko of Japan (1800), Vladimir Komarov, cosmonaut (1927), Bernardo Bertolucci, film director (1941).

17 March

17 March is Saint Patrick's Day. Saint Patrick is the patron saint of Ireland. And on 17 March 1969, Golda Meir became Prime Minister of Israel.

You share a birthday with:
King James IV of Scotland (1473), Rudolf Nureyev, ballet dancer (1938), Kurt Russell, actor (1951).

18 March

On 18 March 1837, Caligula was declared Emperor of Rome. And on 18 March 1965, cosmonaut Aleksei Leonov became the first person to space walk.

You share a birthday with:
Wilfred Owen, poet (1893), John Updike, writer (1932), Queen Latifah, singer (1970).

19 March

On 19 March 1932, the Sydney Harbour Bridge opened. 19 March is also the feast day of Saint Joseph, patron saint of fathers and carpenters.

You share a birthday with:
Wyatt Earp, American gunfighter (1848), Philip Roth, writer (1933), Glenn Close, actress (1947), Bruce Willis, actor (1955).

20 March

On 20 March 1916, Albert Einstein published his theory of relativity. On 20 March 1966, the football World Cup's Jules Rimet trophy was stolen from Central Hall, Westminster, London.

You share a birthday with:
Ovid, Roman poet (43 BC), Napoleon II of France (1811), Henrik Ibsen, writer (1828), Spike Lee, film director (1957), Holly Hunter, actress (1958).

21 March

In 1935, Persia formally changed its name to Iran. And on 21 March 1963, Alcatraz, the famous prison in San Francisco Bay, closed.

You share a birthday with:
Johann Sebastian Bach, composer (1685), Timothy Dalton, James Bond actor (1944), Ronaldinho, Brazilian footballer (1980).

22 March

On 22 March 1888, the English Football League was formed. On 22 March 1993, Intel introduced the Pentium microprocessor.

You share a birthday with:
William Shatner, *Star Trek* actor (1931), Andrew Lloyd Webber, composer (1948), Reese Witherspoon, actress (1976).

23 March

On 23 March 1998, the movie *Titanic* won 11 Oscars at the Academy Awards.

You share a birthday with:
Roger Bannister, runner (1929), Sir Steve Redgrave, Olympic champion rower (1962).

24 March

On 24 March 1603, Queen Elizabeth I died and King James VI of Scotland came to the throne, uniting England and Scotland under a single monarch.

You share a birthday with:
Harry Houdini, escapologist (1874), Steve McQueen, actor (1930), Alyson Hannigan, actress (1974).

25 March
On 25 March 1133, William the Conqueror ordered the Domesday survey of England. And on 25 March 1306, Robert the Bruce was crowned King of Scotland.
You share a birthday with:
Aretha Franklin, singer (1942), Elton John, singer (1947), Sarah Jessica Parker, actress (1965).

26 March
On 26 March 1920, F Scott Fitzgerald's first novel, *This Side of Paradise*, was published.
You share a birthday with:
Tennessee Williams, writer (1911), Diana Ross, singer (1944), Keira Knightley, actress (1985).

27 March
On 27 March 1625, Charles I became King of England and Scotland. On 27 March 1871, the first international rugby match was played between England and Scotland.
You share a birthday with:
King Louis XVII of France (1785), Quentin Tarantino, film director (1963), Sadie Frost, actress (1968), Mariah Carey, singer (1970).

"Summer makes me drowsy,
Autumn makes me sing,
Winter's pretty lousy,
But I hate Spring."
— Dorothy Parker, writer

28 March
On 28 March 1939, the Spanish Civil War ended after three years. On 28 March 1964, the UK's first pirate radio station, Radio Caroline, started transmissions from a ship moored offshore.

You share a birthday with:
Maxim Gorky, Russian writer (1868), Michael Parkinson, talk show host (1935), Nasser Hussain, cricketer (1968), Vince Vaughn, actor (1970).

29 March
On 29 March 1974, the unmanned US spacecraft *Mariner 10* visited the planet Mercury, sending back close-up images of the planet.
You share a birthday with:
John Major, former UK Prime Minister (1943), Elle Macpherson, model (1964).

30 March
On 30 March 1842, Dr Crawford Long used anaesthetic in an operation for the first time.
You share a birthday with:
Anna Sewell, writer of *Black Beauty* (1820), Vincent Van Gogh, artist (1853), Celine Dion, singer (1968).

31 March
On 31 March 1836, the first instalment of *The Pickwick Papers*, Dickens' first novel, was published. And on 31 March 1889, the Eiffel Tower was opened in Paris.
You share a birthday with:
Joseph Haydn, composer (1732), Nikolai Gogol, writer (1809), Christopher Walken, actor (1943), Ewan McGregor, actor (1971).

Daffodil

April

April was probably named after the Latin word meaning *to open*, because leaves and buds start to open in this spring month. Or it might have been named after an ancient goddess of love.

Birthstone: Diamond
Flower: Daisy or sweet pea
Star Signs: Pisces (see page 113) and . . .

Taurus (the Bull)
Dates: 21 April – 21 May
Ruling Planet: Venus
Element: Earth

Does this sound anything like you? If you're born under the sign of Taurus, you're supposed to make a great friend because you're loyal and reliable, and you're also supposed to be practical and persevering. But you might be rather stubborn and find that people accuse you of being materialistic.

April Birthdays

1 April

On 1 April 1918, the British Royal Air Force was founded. 1 April is also April Fool's Day – but don't forget that after midday the joke is on you.

You share a birthday with:
Milan Kundera, writer (1929), Jimmy Cliff, musician (1948), David Gower, cricketer (1957).

2 April

On 2 April 1513, Spanish explorer Juan Ponce de Leon landed in Florida and claimed the area for Spain. On 2 April 1977, Red Rum won the Grand National horse race for a record third time.

You share a birthday with:
Hans Christian Andersen, writer (1805), Emile Zola, writer (1840), Alec Guinness, actor (1914), Marvin Gaye, singer (1939), Linford Christie, athlete (1960).

3 April

On 3 April 1860, the Pony Express mail service began across 2,900 kilometres of America. And on 3 April 1882, the "Wild West" outlaw Jesse James was shot dead by a member of his own gang.

You share a birthday with:
King Philip III of France (1245), Washington Irving, writer (1783), Marlon Brando, actor (1924), Eddie Murphy, comedian and actor (1961).

4 April

On 4 April 1581, Francis Drake was made a knight by Elizabeth I for his circumnavigation of the world. And on 4 April 1968, the civil rights campaigner and preacher Martin Luther King was assassinated in Memphis, Tennessee.

You share a birthday with:
Caracalla, Roman Emperor (186 AD), Maya Angelou, writer (1928), David Blaine, illusionist (1973), Heath Ledger, actor (1979).

5 April

On 5 April 1614, Native American Pocahontas married English tobacco planter, John Rolfe in Jamestown, Virginia, bringing peace between the Jamestown settlers and the Powhatan people.

You share a birthday with:
Bette Davis, actress (1908), Gregory Peck, actor (1916), Agnetha Fältskog, singer with ABBA (1950).

6 April

On 6 April 1896, the Olympic Games took place for the first time in 1,500 years. They were held in Athens, Greece, and were the first modern summer Olympic Games.

You share a birthday with:
Butch Cassidy, US outlaw (1866), John Betjeman, poet (1906), Andre Previn, conductor (1929).

7 April

On 7 April 1795, France made the metre its unit of measurement. And on 7 April 2001, the unmanned spacecraft *Mars Odyssey* was launched on a mission to find evidence of life on Mars.

You share a birthday with:
William Wordsworth, poet (1770), Billie Holiday, jazz singer (1915), Francis Ford Coppola, film director (1939), Jackie Chan, martial arts expert and actor (1954), Russell Crowe, actor (1964).

> "Growing old is mandatory; growing up is optional."
> – Chili Davis, baseball star

8 April

On 8 April 217AD, the Roman Emperor Caracalla was assassinated. On 8 April 1820, the Ancient Greek sculpture known as the Venus de Milo was discovered on the Greek island of Melos (also known as Milos).
You share a birthday with:
King Peter I of Portugal (1320), King Albert I of Belgium (1875), Vivienne Westwood, fashion designer (1941).

9 April

On 9 April 1992, John Major won the UK general election and became Prime Minister. On 9 April 2005, Prince Charles married his second wife, Camilla Parker Bowles.
You share a birthday with:
Charles Baudelaire, poet (1821), Rachel Stevens, singer (1978).

10 April

On 10 April 1912, the RMS *Titanic* set off on its fateful voyage across the Atlantic. And on 10 April 1970, Paul McCartney announced that the Beatles had split up.
You share a birthday with:
William Hazlitt, writer (1778), Vladimir Lenin, Premier of the USSR (1870), Omar Sharif, actor (1932), Haley Joel Osment, actor (1988).

11 April

On 11 April 1814, Napoleon abdicated as Emperor of France and was exiled to the island of Elba.
You share a birthday with:
Septimius Severus, Roman Emperor (146 AD), King John I of Portugal (1357), Joss Stone, singer (1987).

12 April

On 12 April 1961, Soviet cosmonaut Yuri Alekseyevich Gagarin became the first human being to travel into space. On 12 April 1992, Euro Disney opened near Paris, later to be renamed Disneyland Paris.

You share a birthday with:
David Letterman, US talk show host (1947), Tom Clancy, writer (1947), Shannen Doherty, actress (1971), Claire Danes, actress (1979).

13 April

On 13 April 1970, an oxygen tank blew up on the spacecraft *Apollo 13* while on its way to the moon. Fortunately, the three astronauts survived.
You share a birthday with:
Samuel Beckett, writer (1906), Al Green, singer (1946), Garry Kasparov, chess champion (1963).

14 April

On 14 April 1865, US President Abraham Lincoln was fatally shot at the theatre. And on 14 April 1912, *RMS Titanic* hit an iceberg and began to sink.
You share a birthday with:
John Gielgud, actor (1904), Sarah Michelle Gellar, actress (1977).

15 April

On 15 April 1755, Samuel Johnson's *Dictionary of the English Language* was published.
You share a birthday with:
Leonardo da Vinci, artist and inventor (1452), Henry James, writer (1843), Emma Watson, *Harry Potter* actress (1990).

16 April

On 16 April 1972, *Apollo 16* was launched on its successful mission to the moon. And on 16 April 2003, Makobo Modjadji was crowned the new Rain Queen of Balobedu in South Africa.
You share a birthday with:
Wilbur Wright, inventor of the aeroplane (1867), Charlie Chaplin, actor (1889), Kingsley Amis, writer (1922).

17 April

On 17 April 1961, the Bay of Pigs invasion began, when a group of US-trained Cuban exiles landed in Cuba and tried to get rid of Fidel Castro's communist government. (The attack failed.)
You share a birthday with:
Nikita Khrushchev, former Premier of the USSR (1894), Jennifer Garner, actress (1972), Victoria Beckham, singer (1974).

18 April

On 18 April 1025, Boleslaw Chrobry became the first King of Poland. On 18 April 1906, the Great San Francisco Earthquake struck, destroying much of the city.
You share a birthday with:
Ahmed I, Ottoman Emperor (1590), Princess Sayako of Japan (1969), Melissa Joan Hart, actress (1976).

19 April

On 19 April 1775, the American Revolution began with the Battle of Lexington. And on 19 April 2005, Joseph Ratzinger was elected Pope Benedict XVI.
You share a birthday with:
Kate Hudson, actress (1979), Hayden Christensen, actor (1981), Maria Sharapova, tennis player (1987).

Danish Birthdays

If it's your birthday in Denmark, the national flag is flown outside your house so that everyone gets the hint. While you're asleep on the night before your birthday, gifts are sneaked into your bedroom — when you wake up, you're surrounded by birthday presents.

20 April

On 20 April 1841, Edgar Allen Poe's *The Murders in the Rue Morgue*, the first detective story, was published. And on 20 April 1972, *Apollo 16* landed on the moon.
You share a birthday with:
Emperor Go-Komyo of Japan (1633), Adolf Hitler, leader of Germany (1889), Jessica Lange, actress (1949), Carmen Electra, actress (1972).

21 April

On 21 April 753 BC, Rome was founded, according to tradition, by twins Romulus and Remus. And on 21 April 1956, Elvis Presley had his first number one hit record, "Heartbreak Hotel".
You share a birthday with:
Charlotte Brontë, writer (1816), Queen Elizabeth II (1926).

22 April

On 20 April 1509, Henry VIII became King of England on the death of his father, Henry VII.
You share a birthday with:
Yehudi Menuhin, musician (1916), Jack Nicholson, actor (1937), Robert Oppenheimer, physicist (1904).

23 April

On 23 April 1661, Charles II became King of England, Scotland and Ireland. And 23 April is also Saint George's Day. Saint George is the patron saint of England.
You share a birthday with:
King Alfonso II of Portugal (1185), William Shakespeare, writer (1564), Vladimir Nabokov, writer (1899).

24 April

On 24 April 1970, the first Chinese satellite, *Dong Fang Hong I*, was launched. And on 24 April 2005, Cardinal Joseph Ratzinger was inaugurated as Pope Benedict XVI.

You share a birthday with:
Anthony Trollope, writer (1815), Jean-Paul Gaultier, fashion designer (1952), Kelly Clarkson, singer (1982).

25 APRIL

On 25 April 1719, Daniel Defoe's novel *Robinson Crusoe* was published. And on 25 April 1990, the Hubble Space Telescope was put into orbit around Earth and began sending back its first pictures of the universe.

You share a birthday with:
Oliver Cromwell, general (1599), Guglielmo Marconi, inventor (1874), Al Pacino, actor (1939), Renee Zellweger, actress (1969).

26 APRIL

On 26 April 1607, English colonists landed in Virginia and made the first permanent English settlement in North America. And on 26 April 1994, the first multiracial elections in South Africa were held.

You share a birthday with:
King Peter II of Portugal (1648), Eugene Delacroix, artist (1798), Jet Li, actor (1963).

27 APRIL

On 27 April 1124, David I became King of Scotland. And on 27 April 1521, Portuguese explorer Ferdinand Magellan was killed by a poisoned arrow in the Philippine Islands.

You share a birthday with:
Ulysses S Grant, former US President (1822), Coretta Scott King, civil rights activist (1927), Darcey Bussell, ballerina (1969).

28 APRIL

On 28 April 1789, Fletcher Christian led a mutiny on the *HMS Bounty*, and Captain William Bligh and his supporters were set adrift in an open boat.

You share a birthday with:
King Edward IV of England (1442), Terry Pratchett, author (1948), Penelope Cruz, actress (1974).

29 APRIL

On 29 April 1770, explorer Captain Cook arrived in Botany Bay, Australia.

You share a birthday with:
Hirohito, former Emperor of Japan (1901), Daniel Day-Lewis, actor (1957), Michelle Pfeiffer, actress (1958), Uma Thurman, actress (1970).

30 APRIL

On 30 April 711 AD, the Moors landed at Gibraltar and began their invasion of Spain and Portugal. On 30 April 1993, CERN (a European organisation for nuclear research) announced that the World Wide Web would be free to everyone.

You share a birthday with:
Saint Rose of Lima (1586), King Carl Gustav of Sweden (1946), Kirsten Dunst, actress (1982).

Daisy

May

May was named by the Romans, probably after Maia, an Ancient Greek goddess of growth. In the northern hemisphere, May is the month when plants burst into vigorous growth, and perhaps that's why May Day is celebrated in so many countries of the world.

Birthstone: Emerald
Flower: Lily of the Valley or hawthorn
Star Signs: Taurus (see page 119) and . . .

Gemini (the Twins)

Dates: 22 May – 21 June
Ruling Planet: Mercury
Element: Air

Does this sound anything like you? If you're a Geminian, you're supposed to be fun, witty, charming and lively. You're a good communicator but you might get bored easily and find it difficult to concentrate on one thing at a time. Perhaps you could be accused of being fickle, unreliable and even two-faced.

May Birthdays

1 May

On 1 May 1851, the Great Exhibition opened in the Crystal Palace in London and had six million visitors before it closed six months later. And on 1 May 1931, the Empire State Building in New York was officially opened.
You share a birthday with:
Calamity Jane, Wild West Performer (1852), Joseph Heller, writer (1923), Joanna Lumley, actress (1946).

2 May

On 2 May 1933, a sighting of the Loch Ness Monster was reported, starting the modern legend of the creature's existence. On 2 May 1953, King Hussein of Jordan was crowned. And on 2 May 1997 Tony Blair became Prime Minister of Britain, ending eighteen years of Conservative government.
You share a birthday with:
Catherine the Great, Empress of Russia (1729), David Beckham, footballer (1975).

3 May

On 3 May 1494, Christopher Columbus first spotted Jamaica in the West Indies, thinking it was part of India.
You share a birthday with:
Constantine III, Byzantine Emperor (612 AD), Golda Meir, Prime Minister of Israel (1898), James Brown, singer (1928).

4 May

On 4 May 1979, Margaret Thatcher became the first female British Prime Minister.
You share a birthday with:
King Henry I of France (1008), Audrey Hepburn, actress (1929), Keith Haring, artist (1958).

5 May

On 5 May 1821, Napoleon Bonaparte, former Emperor of France, died in exile on the island of Saint Helena.
You share a birthday with:
Karl Marx, political philosopher (1818), Michael Palin, actor (1943), Craig David, singer (1981).

6 May

On 6 May 1954, Roger Bannister became the first person ever to run a mile in under four minutes. And on 6 May 1994 the Channel Tunnel opened, linking Britain and the rest of Europe.
You share a birthday with:
Sigmund Freud, founder of psychoanalysis (1856), Tony Blair, British Prime Minister (1953), George Clooney, actor (1961).

No Pants Day
The first Friday in May is No Pants Day. This is the US version of "pants" and it doesn't mean your undies! The idea is to go trouser-less, dressed in just your knickers. Do you fancy taking part in the celebration?

7 May

On 7 May 1960, Leonid Brezhnev became President of the USSR.
You share a birthday with:
Robert Browning, poet (1812), Johannes Brahms, composer (1833), Peter Tchaikovsky, composer (1840).

8 May

On 8 May 1945, Germany surrendered to the Allies, ending the Second World War in Europe (the date is known as Victory in Europe Day, or VE Day).
You share a birthday with:
Harry S Truman, former US President (1884), Enrique Iglesias, singer (1975).

9 May

On 9 May 1671, Captain Blood stole the crown jewels from the Tower of London and was captured, but managed to impress King Charles II so much that he was pardoned.
You share a birthday with:
J M Barrie, writer of *Peter Pan* (1860), Richard Adams, writer of *Watership Down* (1920), Alan Bennett, playwright (1934), Glenda Jackson, actress and politician (1936), Billy Joel, singer (1949).

10 May

On 10 May 1994, Nelson Mandela became the first black president of South Africa.
You share a birthday with:
Bono, singer (1960), Linda Evangelista, model (1965), Dennis Bergkamp, footballer (1969).

11 May

On 11 May 1812, Spencer Perceval was shot dead, becoming the only British Prime Minister ever to be assassinated.
You share a birthday with:
Salvador Dali, artist (1904), Louis Farrakhan, black rights activist (1933), Holly Valance, actress (1983).

12 May

On May 12 1937, King George VI of the United Kingdom was crowned.
You share a birthday with:
Edward Lear, writer (1812), Florence Nightingale, nurse (1820), Katharine Hepburn, actress (1907).

13 May

On 13 May 1981, Pope John Paul II was shot and seriously wounded in Rome.
You share a birthday with:
Daphne du Maurier, writer (1907), Harvey Keitel, actor (1939), Stevie Wonder, singer (1951).

14 May

On 14 May 1796, Edward Jenner proved the principle of vaccination for the first time, by successfully vaccinating a child against smallpox.
You share a birthday with:
Dante, poet (1265), George Lucas, film director and creator of *Star Wars* (1945), Eoin Colfer, writer (1965), Cate Blanchett, actress (1969).

15 May

On 15 May 1963, Tottenham Hotspur became the first British football club to win a European trophy. And on 15 May 2004 the largest prime number was discovered (it's $2^{24036583} - 1$).
You share a birthday with:
Claudio Monteverdi, composer (1567), L Frank Baum, writer of *The Wizard of Oz* (1856), Andrew Murray, tennis player (1987).

16 May

On 16 May 1770, the French Dauphin Louis married Marie Antoinette – they became King and Queen of France in 1774 and later lost their heads in the French Revolution.
You share a birthday with:
Pierce Brosnan, actor (1953), Olga Korbut, gymnast (1955), Janet Jackson, singer (1966).

17 May

On 17 May 1920, the Dutch airline KLM became the first commercial airline by operating its first scheduled flight from London to Amsterdam.

You share a birthday with:
Alfonso XIII of Spain (1886), Dennis Potter, writer (1935), Dennis Hopper, actor (1936).

18 MAY

On 18 May 1152, Henry II of England married Eleanor of Aquitaine. And on 18 May 1910, the Earth passed through the tail of Halley's Comet.
You share a birthday with:
Bertrand Russell, philosopher (1872), Pope John Paul II (1920), Chow Yun-Fat, actor (1955).

19 MAY

On 19 May 1536, Anne Boleyn, the second wife of King Henry VIII, was beheaded. And on 19 May 1897, Oscar Wilde was released from Reading jail after serving two years hard labour for "gross indecency" (he was homosexual).
You share a birthday with:
Ho Chi-Minh, former leader of Vietnam (1892), Malcolm X, political activist (1925), Nora Ephron, film director (1941), Victoria Wood, comedian (1953).

20 MAY

On 20 May 1498, Vasco da Gama became the first European explorer to reach India. And on 20 May 1536, Henry VIII married his third wife, Jane Seymour.
You share a birthday with:
Honoré de Balzac, writer (1799), John Stuart Mill, philosopher (1806), Cher, singer (1946), Busta Rhymes, rapper (1972).

Marry in May?
It's not a good idea to get married in May — an old rhyme says:
"Marry in the month of May
And you'll surely rue the day."

21 MAY

On 21 May 1927, American pilot Charles Lindbergh landed at Le Bourget airfield in Paris, successfully completing the first ever nonstop flight between New York and Paris.
You share a birthday with:
Alexander Pope, poet (1688), Henri Rousseau, artist (1844), Andrei Sakharov, physicist (1921), Notorious BIG, rapper (1972).

22 MAY

On 22 May 1455, the Yorkists defeated King Henry VI's Lancastrian army in the first battle of England's Wars of the Roses.
You share a birthday with:
Richard Wagner, composer (1813), Sir Arthur Conan Doyle, *Sherlock Holmes* writer (1859), Laurence Olivier, actor (1907), George Best, footballer, (1946), Naomi Campbell, model (1970), Katie Price (Jordan), model (1978).

23 MAY

In Ancient Rome, 23 May was a festival day in honour of Vulcan, the god of fire and metalworking. On 23 May 1701, Captain Kidd, the famous pirate, was hanged for piracy and murder.
You share a birthday with:
King Philip I of France (1052), Joan Collins, actress (1933), Jewel, singer (1974).

24 MAY

On 24 May 1844, inventor Samuel Morse made the first transmission on the world's first commercial telegraph line. On 24 May 1956, the Eurovision Song Contest was held for the first time.
You share a birthday with:
Bob Dylan, singer (1941), Priscilla Presley, actress and wife of Elvis (1945).

25 MAY

On 25 May 1660, Charles II, the exiled King of England, returned to England to restore the monarchy. And on 25 May 1977, the movie *Star Wars* was first released.
You share a birthday with:
Anne Brontë, writer (1820), Ian McKellen, actor (1939), Frank Oz, actor and *Muppets* puppeteer (1944), Mike Myers, actor and comedian (1963).

26 MAY

On 26 May 1896, Nicholas II was crowned Tsar of Russia. And on 26 May 1897, Bram Stoker's novel *Dracula* was published.
You share a birthday with:
Alexandr Pushkin, writer (1799), John Wayne, actor (1907), Alan Hollinghurst, writer (1954), Helena Bonham Carter, actress (1966).

27 MAY

On 27 May 1703, the Russian city of St Petersburg was founded by Peter the Great. And on 27 May 1937, San Francisco's Golden Gate Bridge opened.
You share a birthday with:
Wild Bill Hickok, US outlaw (1837), Christopher Lee, actor (1922), Paul Bettany, actor (1971), Jamie Oliver, chef (1975).

28 MAY

On 28 May 1533, Henry VIII married his second wife, Anne Boleyn. 28 May is also the feast day of Saint Bernard of Menthon, patron saint of mountaineers, after whom the St Bernard dog is named.
You share a birthday with:
John the Fearless of Burgundy (1371), King George I of Great Britain (1660), Ian Fleming, *James Bond* writer (1908), Kylie Minogue, singer (1968).

29 MAY

On 29 May 1953, Mount Everest was climbed for the first time ever by New Zealander Edmund Hillary and Nepalese Tenzing Norgay.
You share a birthday with:
King Charles II of England (1630), Tenzing Norgay, the explorer who climbed Everest on this day in 1953 (1914), John F Kennedy, former US President (1917), Noel Gallagher, musician (1967).

30 MAY

On 30 May 1971, the unmanned space probe *Mariner 9* was launched on a mission to gather information about Mars. It is also the feast day of Saint Joan of Arc, who was burned at the stake on this day in 1431.
You share a birthday with:
Peter the Great, Tsar of Russia (1672), Steven Gerrard, footballer (1980).

31 MAY

On 31 May 1669, Samuel Pepys made the last entry in his famous diary. On 31 May 1859, Big Ben, the famous bell in the clock tower of the House of Commons, rang for the very first time.
You share a birthday with:
Omar Khayyam, poet, astronomer and philosopher (1048), Clint Eastwood, actor and film director (1930), Colin Farrell, actor (1976).

Lily of the Valley

June

June was named after the Roman goddess Juno, the queen of the gods and goddess of women and marriage, and there was a festival in her honour at the beginning of the month. The Romans thought June was the best month to get married.

Birthstone: Pearl
Flower: Rose
Star Signs: Gemini (see page 125) and . . .

Cancer (the Crab)
Dates: 22 June – 22 July
Ruling Planet: Moon
Element: Water

Does this sound anything like you? If you're a Cancerian, you're supposed to love home life and caring for others. You're also supposed to have a good memory. On the downside, you might also tend to be moody and sulky.

June Birthdays

1 JUNE

On 1 June 1910, Captain Scott set off on an expedition to be the first to the South Pole. And in 1938, Superman, created by US students Joseph Shuster and Jerry Siegel, made his first appearance in *Action Comics #1*. *You share a birthday with:*
Marilyn Monroe, actress (1926), Morgan Freeman, actor (1937), Heidi Klum, model (1973), Alanis Morissette, singer (1974).

2 JUNE

On 2 June 1953, Queen Elizabeth II was crowned Queen of the United Kingdom.
You share a birthday with:
Thomas Hardy, writer (1840), Edward Elgar, composer (1857), Johnny Weissmuller, Olympic swimmer and TV *Tarzan* (1904).

3 JUNE

On this day in 1937, Edward, Duke of Windsor, married Mrs Wallis Simpson. He had formerly been King Edward III, but had given up the throne because he had fallen in love with a divorcee.
You share a birthday with:
King George V of the United Kingdom (1865), Raoul Dufy, artist (1877), Allen Ginsberg, poet (1926).

4 JUNE

On 4 June 1783 in France, the Montgolfier brothers gave the first public demonstration of their latest invention, the hot air balloon. On 4 June 1917, Suffragette Emily Davison ran out in front of the King's horse at the Derby horse race. She died of her injuries a few days later.
You share a birthday with:
Socrates, ancient Greek philosopher (470 BC), King George III of Great Britain (1738), Angelina Jolie, actress (1975).

5 JUNE

On 5 June 1915, Danish women were given the right to vote. 5 June is also World Environment Day.
You share a birthday with:
Pancho Villa, Mexican revolutionary (1878), Margaret Drabble, writer (1939), Ken Follett, writer (1949), "Marky" Mark Wahlberg, actor (1971).

6 JUNE

6 June 1944, became known as D-Day, when more than 150,000 British, US and Canadian troops landed on the beaches of Normandy in northern France – the beginning of the Allied invasion of Europe that led to victory in World War II.
You share a birthday with:
King John III of Portugal (1502), Captain Robert Falcon Scott, explorer (1868), Bjorn Borg, tennis player (1956).

7 JUNE

On this day in 1329, King Robert I of Scotland, better known as Robert the Bruce, died. On 7 June 1929, Vatican City became a state – the smallest independent nation in the world.
You share a birthday with:
Paul Gauguin, artist (1848), Liam Neeson, actor (1952), Anna Kournikova, tennis player (1981).

8 JUNE

On 8 June 68 AD, Galba became Emperor of Rome. And on 8 June 1949, George Orwell's *Nineteen Eighty-Four* was published.
You share a birthday with:
Frank Lloyd Wright, architect (1867), Tim Berners-Lee, inventor of the Worldwide Web (1955).

Lithuanian Birthdays

If it's your birthday in Lithuania you might find yourself wearing a birthday sash and sitting in a specially decorated chair, which will be lifted up three times by your friends and family in honour of your birthday. The door of your house will be decorated with flowers, too.

9 JUNE

On this day in 1898, the UK signed an agreement to lease Hong Kong from China for ninety-nine years. On 9 June 1934, Donald Duck made his first screen appearance.
You share a birthday with:
George Stephenson, inventor (1781), Johnny Depp, actor (1963), Natalie Portman, actress (1981).

10 JUNE

On 10 June 1829, the first boat race between Oxford and Cambridge was held. And on 10 June 2003, the *Spirit Rover* was launched on NASA mission to Mars.
You share a birthday with:
Judy Garland, actress (1922), Elizabeth Hurley, actress (1965).

11 JUNE

On 11 June 1509, King Henry VIII of England married his first wife, Catherine of Aragon. And on 11 June 1962, three men escaped from the famous Alcatraz prison in San Francisco.
You share a birthday with:
Ben Jonson, poet and dramatist (1572), John Constable, artist (1776), Richard Strauss, composer (1864).

12 JUNE

On 12 June 1898, the Philippines became independent after 300 years of Spanish rule. And on 12 June 1991, Boris Yeltsin was elected President of Russia.
You share a birthday with:
Egon Schiele, artist (1890), Anne Frank, diarist (1929).

13 JUNE

On 13 June 1381, a peasant army led by Wat Tyler marched into London, in the Peasants' Revolt.
You share a birthday with:
James Clerk Maxwell, physicist (1831), W B Yeats, poet (1865), Mary-Kate and Ashley Olsen, actresses (1986).

14 JUNE

In the USA this is Flag Day, celebrating the adoption of the Stars and Stripes as the national flag on this day in 1777. And on 14 June 1982, the Falklands War ended when Argentina surrendered to Britain.
You share a birthday with:
Che Guevara, Argentinian revolutionary (1928), Donald Trump, businessman (1946), Boy George, singer and DJ (1961), Steffi Graf, tennis player (1969).

15 JUNE

On 15 June 1215, King John of England signed the Magna Carta.
You share a birthday with:
Simon Callow, actor (1949), Courteney Cox, actress (1964), Ice Cube, rapper (1969).

16 JUNE

On 16 June 1963, Soviet cosmonaut Valentina Tereshkova became the first

woman to travel into space. And every 16 June, Bloomsday is celebrated in Dublin, when people enact and read from James Joyce's famous novel *Ulysses*, set in the city.
You share a birthday with:
Murad IV, Ottoman Sultan (1612), King Gustav V of Sweden (1858), Stan Laurel, actor and comedian (1890), Tupac Shakur, rapper (1971).

17 JUNE

On 17 June 1579, Sir Francis Drake claimed California for England during his circumnavigation of the world, calling it Nova Albion.
You share a birthday with:
King Edward I of England (1239), Igor Stravinsky, composer (1882), Venus Williams, tennis player (1980), Lee Ryan, singer (1983).

18 JUNE

On 18 June 1815, Napoleon Bonaparte was defeated by the Duke of Wellington at the Battle of Waterloo.
You share a birthday with:
Paul McCartney, singer (1942), Isabella Rossellini, actress (1952).

19 JUNE

On 19 June 1885, the Statue of Liberty arrived in the harbour of New York City. On this day in 1862, slavery became illegal in US territories.
You share a birthday with:
King James I of England and VI of Scotland (1566), Blaise Pascal, mathematician (1623), Salman Rushdie, writer (1947).

20 JUNE

On 20 June 1837, Queen Victoria became Queen of the United Kingdom.
You share a birthday with:
King Sigismund I of Sweden (1561), Nicole Kidman, actress (1967), Frank Lampard, footballer (1978).

21 JUNE

On 21 June 2003, *Harry Potter and the Order of the Phoenix* by J K Rowling was published (the fifth book in the series). 21 June is also the summer solstice, the longest day of the year.
You share a birthday with:
Jean-Paul Sartre, philosopher (1905), Prince William of the United Kingdom (1982).

22 JUNE

On 22 June 1911, George V was crowned King of the United Kingdom. Liverpool's Royal Liver Clock, known as "Great George", was started at the exact moment of the coronation.
You share a birthday with:
Meryl Streep, actress (1949), Dan Brown, writer of *The Da Vinci Code* (1964).

23 JUNE

23 June is Midsummer Eve or Midsummer Night. In ancient times, people celebrated it by lighting bonfires and dancing round them and by holding torchlit processions.
You share a birthday with:
Pharaoh Ptolemy XV of Egypt (47 BC), King Edward VIII of the United Kingdom (1894), Alan Turing, mathematician (1912), Patrick Viera, footballer (1976).

24 JUNE

On 24 June 1812, Napoleon's army invaded Russia. And on 24 June 1901, the first major exhibition of Pablo Picasso's art was held in Paris. The painter was just nineteen.
You share a birthday with:
Saint John of the Cross (1542), Betty Jackson, fashion designer (1949).

> "A birthday is just the first day of another 365-day journey around the sun. Enjoy the trip."
> — Unknown

25 JUNE

25 June 1876 is the date of Custer's Last Stand at Little Big Horn.
You share a birthday with:
George Orwell, writer (1903), George Michael, singer (1963).

26 JUNE

On 26 June 1541, Francisco Pizarro, the Spanish conqueror of the Incas, was assassinated. On 26 June 1977, Elvis Presley gave his last ever concert. And on 26 June 1997, *Harry Potter and the Philosopher's Stone*, the first book in the series, was published.
You share a birthday with:
Lord Kelvin, physicist (1824), Laurie Lee, writer (1914), Princess Alexia of the Netherlands (2005).

27 JUNE

On 27 June 1898, Canadian Joshua Slocum became the first person to sail around the world single-handed.
You share a birthday with:
King Louis XII of France (1462), Helen Keller, blind and deaf writer and teacher (1880), Tobey Maguire, actor (1975).

28 JUNE

On 28 June 1914, Archduke Franz Ferdinand, heir to the Austro-Hungarian empire, was assassinated, leading to the start of the First World War.
You share a birthday with:
King Henry VIII of England (1491), Mel Brooks, actor and director (1926), Kathy Bates, actress (1948), John Cusack, actor (1966).

29 JUNE

On 29 June 1613, Shakespeare's Globe Theatre in London was destroyed by fire. And on 29 June 1986, Argentina won the football World Cup.
You share a birthday with:
King John II of Aragon (1397), Prince Bernhard of the Netherlands (1911), Pedro Santana Lopez, Prime Minister of Portugal (1956), Amanda Donohoe, actress (1962).

30 JUNE

On 30 June 1859, Frenchman Emile Blondin walked across a tightrope suspended fifty metres above Niagara Falls. And on 30 June 1960, the Congo became independent from Belgium.
You share a birthday with:
King Charles VIII of France (1470), "Iron" Mike Tyson, boxer (1966).

Rose

July

July is named after Julius Caesar, the ruler of Rome. He reorganised the Roman calendar and decided to name a month after himself (he wasn't famous for his modesty). He chose the month of his birthday, naturally. In Britain, the month used to be pronounced like the name Julie because of its association with Julius Caesar.

Birthstone: Ruby
Flower: Delphinium
Star Signs: Cancer (see page 131) and . . .

Leo (the Lion)
Dates: 22 July – 23 August
Ruling Planet: Sun
Element: Fire

Does this sound anything like you? If you're born under the sign of Leo, you're supposed to be generous, warm-hearted, creative and enthusiastic. But you might also tend to be bossy and intolerant of other people's mistakes.

July Birthdays

1 JULY

On 1 July 1960, Somalia became independent. And on 1 July 1962, Rwanda and Burundi also became independent countries.

You share a birthday with:
Amy Johnson, aviator (1903), Diana, Princess of Wales (1961), Pamela Andersen, actress (1967), Missy Elliott, singer (1971), Ruud Van Nistelrooy, footballer (1976), Liv Tyler, actress (1977).

2 JULY

On 2 July 1937, aviator Amelia Earhart and her navigator went missing as they crossed the Pacific in their plane on a round-the-world trip, and were never seen again. On 2 July 2002, Steve Fossett became the first person to circumnavigate the Earth alone in a balloon. On 2 July 2005, ten Live 8 concerts were held around the world.

You share a birthday with:
Valentinian III, Roman Emperor (419 AD), Jerry Hall, model (1960), Lindsay Lohan, actress (1986).

3 JULY

On 3 July 1928, John Logie Baird made the world's first colour television transmission from Covent Garden in London. On 3 July 1994, Pete Sampras won the men's final at Wimbledon.

You share a birthday with:
Tom Stoppard, playwright (1937), Tom Cruise, actor (1962).

4 JULY

On 4 July 1776, the United States of America issued the Declaration of Independence (from Great Britain). On 4 July 1997, the spacecraft *Pathfinder* landed on Mars.

You share a birthday with:
Murat III, Ottoman Sultan (1546), Guiseppe Garibaldi, Italian patriot (1807), Thomas Barnardo, founder of children's homes (1845).

5 JULY

On 5 July 1946, the bikini was modelled for the first time. It was designed by Louis Reard and named after the atomic tests that took place at Bikini Atoll in the Pacific the same week.

You share a birthday with:
Jean Cocteau, writer (1889), Georges Pompidou, former President of France (1911), Dolly the sheep, the first cloned animal (1996).

6 JULY

On 6 July 1885, Louis Pasteur tested his rabies vaccine on a boy who had been bitten by a rabid dog – it worked. On 6 July each year in Spain, the Pamplona Bull Run takes place, when people run through the streets chased by six stampeding bulls!

You share a birthday with:
Frida Kahlo, artist (1907), Dalai Lama, leader of Tibet (1935), George W Bush, US President (1946), Sylvester Stallone, actor (1946), 50 Cent, singer (1976).

Ruby Superstitions

July's birthstone, the ruby, is supposed to have all sorts of magical properties: it changes colour according to the wearer's health; it brings love; it's a charm against storms and floods; and it's an antidote to snake poison!

7 July

On 7 July 1456, Joan of Arc was acquitted of heresy – unfortunately, she'd been burned at the stake for the crime twenty-five years before.

You share a birthday with:
Emperor Shirakawa of Japan (1053), Marc Chagall, artist (1887), Ringo Starr, musician (1940).

8 July

On 8 July 1947, there were reports of a UFO crash landing in Roswell, New Mexico, USA. And on 8 July 2000, *Harry Potter and the Goblet of Fire* by J K Rowling was published.

You share a birthday with:
Anjelica Huston, actress (1951), Kevin Bacon, actor (1958), Beck, singer (1970).

9 July

On 9 July 1877, the first lawn tennis tournament at Wimbledon began. And on 9 July 1941, the secret code used by the German army, Enigma, was broken by British code breakers.

You share a birthday with:
David Hockney, artist (1937), Tom Hanks, actor (1956), Courtney Love, musician (1965).

10 July

On 10 July 1940, the Battle of Britain, a series of bombing raids agains Britain in the Second World War, began.

You share a birthday with:
Emperor Go-Hanazono of Japan (1419), King James III of Scotland (1452), Marcel Proust, writer (1871), Jessica Simpson, singer and actress (1980).

11 July

On 11 July 1776, Captain James Cook began his third voyage of exploration. On 11 July 1859, *A Tale of Two Cities* by Charles Dickens was published.

You share a birthday with:
Robert the Bruce, King of Scotland (1274), E B White, writer of *Charlotte's Web* (1899), Giorgio Armani, fashion designer (1935).

12 July

On 12 July 1543, Henry VIII married his sixth and final wife, Catherine Parr.

You share a birthday with:
Julius Caesar, ruler of Rome (100 BC), King Louis II of Monaco (1870), Bill Cosby, actor and comedian (1937).

13 July

On 13 July 1985, the Live Aid concert began at Wembley Stadium in London to raise money for famine victims in Africa.

You share a birthday with:
Ferdinand III, Holy Roman Emperor (1608), Harrison Ford, actor (1942), Erno Rubik, inventor of the Rubik's cube and other puzzles (1944).

14 July

On 14 July, revolutionaries stormed the Bastille prison in Paris, marking the beginning of the French Revolution.

You share a birthday with:
Emmeline Pankhurst, women's rights campaigner (1858), Gerald Ford, former US President (1913), Gustav Klimt, artist (1918), Ingmar Bergman, film director (1918).

15 July

On 15 July 1965, the unmanned US spacecraft *Mariner 4* sent the first images of the planet Mars. 15 July is also Saint Swithin's Day. Folklore says that if it rains on Saint Swithin's Day, it will rain for forty more days afterwards.

You share a birthday with:
Inigo Jones, architect (1573), Rembrandt, artist (1606), Iris Murdoch, writer (1919).

16 July
On 16 July 1951, *The Catcher in the Rye* by J D Salinger was published. And on 16 July 1969, *Apollo 11*, was launched on the first lunar mission.
You share a birthday with:
Roald Amundsen, polar explorer (1872), Michael Flatley, Irish dancer (1958), Fatboy Slim, musician (1963).

17 July
On 17 July 1762, Catherine the Great became Tsarina of Russia. On 17 July 1955, Disneyland opened for the first time.
You share a birthday with:
Donald Sutherland, actor (1934), David Hasselhoff, actor (1952).

18 July
On 18 July 64 AD, a fire started in Rome. It quickly spread and destroyed most of the city. And on 18 July 1936, the Spanish Civil War began.
You share a birthday with:
William Makepeace Thackeray, novelist (1811), Nelson Mandela, South African President (1918), Richard Branson, entrepreneur (1950), Vin Diesel, actor (1967).

Hong Kong Birthdays
If it's your birthday in Hong Kong you'll get extra-long noodles for your lunch, to symbolise a long life.

19 July
On 19 July 1545, one of King Henry VIII's finest fighting ships, the *Mary Rose*, sank off Portsmouth.
You share a birthday with:
Edgar Degas, artist (1834), Alice Dunbar Nelson, writer (1875).

20 July
On 20 July 1969, *Apollo 11* was the first manned spacecraft to land on the moon. Astronauts Neil Armstrong and Buzz Aldrin became the first people to walk on its surface.
You share a birthday with:
Petrarch, Italian poet (1304), Sir Edmund Hillary, Everest mountaineer (1919), Diana Rigg, actress (1938).

21 July
On 21 July 1994, Tony Blair won the leadership of the Labour Party (he became Prime Minister of Britain three years later).
You share a birthday with:
Ernest Hemingway, novelist (1899), Robin Williams, actor (1952), Josh Hartnett, actor (1978).

22 July
On 22 July 1298, Edward I of England defeated the Scots, led by William Wallace, at the Battle of Falkirk.
You share a birthday with:
Gregor Mendel, father of genetics (1822), Willem Dafoe, actor (1955), Rufus Wainwright, actor (1973).

23 July
On 23 July 1986, Prince Andrew married Sarah Ferguson at Westminster Abbey.
You share a birthday with:
Philip the Handsome, King of Spain (1478), Raymond Chandler, writer (1888), Haile Selassie, Emperor of Ethiopia (1892), Daniel Radcliffe, *Harry Potter* actor (1989).

24 July
On 24 July 1567, Mary Queen of Scots was forced to give up the throne in favour of her one-year-old son, later crowned King James VI of Scotland.
You share a birthday with:
Alexandre Dumas, writer (1802), Amelia Earhart, aviator (1897), Jennifer Lopez, actress (1971).

July

> "Never be the first to arrive at a party or the last to go home, and never, ever be both."
> — David Brown

25 July
On 25 July 1909, Louis Bleriot made the first aeroplane flight across the English Channel. And on 25 July 1978, the world's first "test-tube" baby was born in England.
You share a birthday with:
Alfonso the Conqueror, King of Portugal (1109), Matt LeBlanc, actor (1967).

26 July
On 26 July 1847, Liberia became an independent country. On 26 July 1908, the Federal Bureau of Investigation (FBI) was founded.
You share a birthday with:
George Bernard Shaw, playwright (1856), Carl Jung, psychoanalyst (1875), Mick Jagger, singer (1943), Kevin Spacey, actor and director (1959), Sandra Bullock, actress (1964), Kate Beckinsale, actress (1973).

27 July
On 27 July 1794, Maximilien Robespierre, the leader of the French Revolution's Reign of Terror, was arrested. He was later guillotined. And on 27 July 1940 Bugs Bunny appeared on screen for the first time.
You share a birthday with:
Hilaire Belloc, writer (1870), Bharati Mukherjee, writer (1940).

28 July
On 28 July 1540, Henry VIII married his fifth wife, Catherine Howard. On 28 July 1959, postcodes were introduced in the UK.
You share a birthday with:
Ludwig Feuerbach, philosopher (1804), Beatrix Potter, writer (1866), Jacqueline Kennedy Onassis, former First Lady of the USA (1929).

29 July
On 29 July 1588, the Spanish Armada was defeated by the English navy, led by Francis Drake. On 29 July 1954, *The Fellowship of the Ring*, the first part of *The Lord of the Rings*, was published. And on 29 July 1981, Prince Charles married Lady Diana Spencer.
You share a birthday with:
Benito Mussolini, Italian dictator (1883), Fernando Alonso, racing car driver (1981).

30 July
On 30 July 1966, England, the host nation, won the World Cup in the first televised World Cup.
You share a birthday with:
Emily Brontë, writer of *Wuthering Heights* (1818), Arnold Schwarzenegger, actor and politician (1947), Hilary Swank, actress (1974).

31 July
On 31 July 1498, Christopher Columbus became the first European to land on Trinidad.
You share a birthday with:
Primo Levi, writer (1919), Wesley Snipes, actor (1962), J K Rowling, writer (1965).

Delphinium

August

August was originally the sixth month in the Roman calendar (with March as the first month) and called "Sixtilis", but Emperor Augustus Caesar, the first Roman Emperor, changed that when he thought of a much better name for the month – his own!

Birthstone: Peridot (a yellow-green gemstone)
Flower: Poppy
Star Signs: Leo (see page 137) and . . .

Virgo (the Virgin)
Dates: 24 August – 23 September
Ruling Planet: Mercury
Element: Earth

Does this sound anything like you? If you're born under the sign of Virgo, you're supposed to be intelligent, a perfectionist, and good at arts and crafts. You might be shy and quiet, but you make a great mate because you're sympathetic and always ready to help. You might find you're sometimes accused of being fussy and over-critical.

August Birthdays

1 August

On 1 August 1498, Christopher Columbus landed on the American mainland, in present-day Venezuela. On this day in 1774, Joseph Priestley discovered a gas which later became known as oxygen.

You share a birthday with:
Claudius I, Emperor of Rome (10 BC), Herman Melville, writer (1819), Yves Saint Laurent, fashion designer (1936).

2 August

On 2 August 216 BC, the Carthaginian general Hannibal defeated the Roman army at the Battle of Cannae.

You share a birthday with:
Wes Craven, horror film director (1939), Isabelle Allende, writer (1942).

3 August

On 3 August 1492, Columbus set sail on a journey to find a western sea route to China. And on 3 August 1958, the US nuclear submarine *Nautilus* made the first undersea voyage to the North Pole.

You share a birthday with:
King Friedrich Wilhelm III of Prussia (1770), Rupert Brooke, war poet (1887), P D James, writer (1920), Martin Sheen, actor (1940).

4 August

4 August 1693 is the date traditionally given for the invention of champagne by Dom Perignon. And on 4 August 1902, the Greenwich foot tunnel opened under the River Thames in London.

You share a birthday with:
Percy Bysshe Shelley, poet (1792), Queen Elizabeth the Queen Mother (1900), Louis Armstrong, musician (1901), Billy Bob Thornton, actor (1955).

5 August

On 5 August 1100, Henry I was crowned King of England in Westminster Abbey. On 5 August 1914, the first electric traffic lights were installed in Cleveland, Ohio.

You share a birthday with:
Guy de Maupassant, writer (1850), Neil Armstrong, astronaut (1930).

6 August

On 6 August 1926, Harry Houdini performed his greatest feat, spending ninety-one minutes underwater in a sealed tank before escaping.

You share a birthday with:
Alfred Lord Tennyson, poet (1809), Alexander Fleming, scientist (1881), Andy Warhol, artist (1928), Michelle Yeoh, actress (1962), Geri Halliwell, singer (1972).

7 August

On 7 August 1960, Côte d'Ivoire (the Ivory Coast) became independent from France.

You share a birthday with:
Mata Hari, spy (1876), David Duchovny, actor (1970), Charlize Theron, actress (1975).

8 August

On 8 August 117 AD, Hadrian became Emperor of Rome. On 8 August 1963, the Great Train Robbery took place. On 8 August 1974, Richard Nixon became the first US President to resign.

You share a birthday with:
Emiliano Zapata, Mexican revolutionary (1879), Dustin Hoffman, actor (1937), Chris Eubank, boxer (1966), Princess Beatrice, daughter of Prince Andrew and Sarah Ferguson, Duchess of York (1988).

9 August

On 9 August 1483, the Sistine Chapel in Rome was opened.

You share a birthday with:
John Dryden, poet (1631), Philip Larkin,

poet (1922), Melanie Griffith, actress (1957), Whitney Houston, singer (1963).

10 August
On 10 August 1519, Ferdinand Magellan's five ships set off to be the first to circumnavigate the world. And on 10 August 1990, the Magellan space probe reached Venus.
You share a birthday with:
Herbert Hoover, former US President (1874), Rosanna Arquette, actress (1959), Antonio Banderas, actor (1960).

11 August
On 11 August 480 BC, the Persians defeated the Spartans in the Battle of Thermopylae. And on 11 August 1934, the famous prison at Alcatraz in San Francisco Bay was opened.
You share a birthday with:
Enid Blyton, writer (1897), Hulk Hogan, wrestler and actor (1953).

12 August
On 12 August 1961, East Germany began building the Berlin Wall to divide East and West Berlin.
You share a birthday with:
Tsar Alexei I of Russia (1629), King Alfonso VI of Portugal (1643), Pete Sampras, tennis player (1971).

13 August
On 13 August 1521, Tenochtitlán, the capital city of the Aztec empire, was captured by Spanish forces led by Hernán Cortés.
You share a birthday with:
John Logie Baird, inventor (1888), Alfred Hitchcock, film director (1899), Fidel Castro, President of Cuba (1927).

14 August
On 14 August 1040 the real-life Macbeth killed his cousin, King Duncan of Scotland, in battle.

You share a birthday with:
Steve Martin, actor (1945), Halle Berry, actress (1966).

15 August
On 15 August 1057 at the Battle of Lumphanan, Malcolm Canmore killed King Macbeth of Scotland.
You share a birthday with:
Napoleon I, Emperor of France (1769), Princess Anne (1950), Ben Affleck, actor (1972).

> **What a Bash!**
> The Sultan of Brunei held the world's most expensive birthday party to celebrate his fiftieth birthday on 13 July 1996. The cost was over $27 million! Three Michael Jackson concerts accounted for $16 million of the bill.

16 August
On 16 August 1977, Elvis Presley died at his mansion in Memphis, Tennessee.
You share a birthday with:
Ted Hughes, poet (1930), Madonna, singer (1958).

17 August
On 17 August 1978, the *Double Eagle II* completed the first transatlantic balloon flight.
You share a birthday with:
Davy Crockett, US frontiersman (1786), Robert de Niro, actor (1943), Sean Penn, actor (1960).

18 August

On 18 August 1227, Genghis Khan, the Mongol leader, died in his camp during a campaign.

You share a birthday with:
Roman Polanski, film director (1933), Robert Redford, actor and film director (1937), Patrick Swayze, actor (1954), Edward Norton, actor (1969), Christian Slater, actor (1969).

19 August

On 19 August 1960, the Soviet Union launched the spacecraft *Sputnik 5* containing two dogs, two rats and forty mice. It returned the next day with all of the animals unharmed.

You share a birthday with:
Orville Wright, inventor (1871), Coco Chanel, fashion designer and perfumier (1883), Bill Clinton, former US President (1946), Matthew Perry, actor (1969).

20 August

On 20 August 1940, exiled Russian revolutionary Leon Trotsky was assassinated in Mexico. And on 20 August 1975, the unmanned space probe *Viking 1* was launched on a mission to Mars.

You share a birthday with:
Don King, boxing promoter (1931), Isaac Hayes, singer and actor (1942), Rajiv Gandhi, former Indian Prime Minister (1944), Robert Plant, singer (1948).

21 August

On 21 August 1911, Leonardo da Vinci's painting the *Mona Lisa* was stolen from the Louvre. It was only found two years later.

You share a birthday with:
King Philip II of France (1165), Kim Cattrall, actress (1956), Carrie-Anne Moss, actress (1967).

22 August

On 22 August 1485, Richard III of England was killed at the Battle of Bosworth Field, the last battle in the Wars of the Roses.

You share a birthday with:
Joseph Strauss, composer (1827), Claude Debussy, composer (1862), Tori Amos, singer (1963).

23 August

On 23 August 1305, Scottish hero William Wallace was executed by the English. And on 23 August 1328, Philip VI was crowned King of France.

You share a birthday with:
Gene Kelly, tap dancer and actor (1912), Dick Bruna, illustrator and creator of Miffy (1927), Queen Noor of Jordan (1951), River Phoenix, actor (1970).

24 August

On 24 August 79 AD, Mount Vesuvius erupted, destroying the Roman towns of Pompeii and Herculaneum.

You share a birthday with:
Jorge Luis Borges, writer (1899), Yasser Arafat, Palestinian leader (1929), A S Byatt, writer (1936).

25 August

On 25 August 1875, Englishman Matthew Webb became the first person to swim the English Channel. And on 25 August 1944, Paris was liberated after four years of Nazi occupation.

You share a birthday with:
Ivan the Terrible, Tsar of Russia (1530), Sir Henry Morgan, pirate (1635), Leonard Bernstein, composer (1918), Sean Connery, actor (1930), Claudia Schiffer, model (1970).

26 August

On 26 August 1346, England defeated France at the Battle of Crecy in the Hundred Years War.

You share a birthday with:
Robert Walpole, first British Prime Minister (1676), Macaulay Culkin, actor (1980).

27 AUGUST

On 27 August 55 BC, Julius Caesar invaded Britain. On 27 August 1896, war was declared between Britain and Zanzibar at 9.02 a.m., but ended thirty-eight minutes later, making it the shortest war ever.
You share a birthday with:
Gerhard Berger, racing driver (1959), Mother Teresa of Calcutta (1910).

28 AUGUST

On 28 August 1963, Martin Luther King Junior made his famous "I have a dream" civil rights speech.
You share a birthday with:
Leo Tolstoy, writer (1828), Janet Frame, writer (1924), David Soul, actor and singer (1944), Shania Twain, singer (1965), Jack Black, actor (1969).

29 AUGUST

On 29 August 1533, in Peru, Spanish conquistador Francisco Pizarro executed the last Incan Emperor, Atahuallpa. On 29 August 1833, slavery was abolished in the British Empire. And on 29 August 1896, chop suey was invented in New York City.
You share a birthday with:
Ingrid Berman, actress (1915), Elliot Gould, actor (1938), Michael Jackson, singer (1958).

30 AUGUST

On 30 August 30 BC, Cleopatra, Queen of Egypt, committed suicide following the defeat of her forces against Octavian.
You share a birthday with:
Mary Wollstonecraft Shelley, writer of *Frankenstein* (1797), Cameron Diaz, actress (1972), Andy Roddick, tennis player (1982).

31 AUGUST

On 31 August 1997, Princess Diana died in a car crash in Paris.
You share a birthday with:
Caligula, Roman Emperor (12 AD), Van Morrison, musician (1945).

A Nice Little Earner

The song "Happy Birthday to You" is protected by copyright. But don't worry — it doesn't mean you have to get permission or pay money to sing it on your granny's birthday. You only have to do that if you're planning on singing it at a public event or on telly, in a film or on the radio — yes, there really is an agency that gets paid every time someone does that.

Poppy

September

September's name comes from the Latin word for "seven" – although now it's the ninth month, not the seventh, after changes were made to the calendar. In Britain in 1752, September didn't have days three to thirteen because of the change to the Gregorian calendar – which must have been annoying if one of those days was your birthday.

Birthstone: Sapphire
Flower: Aster or morning glory
Star Signs: Virgo (see page 143) and . . .

Libra (the Scales)
Dates: 24 September – 23 October
Ruling Planet: Venus
Element: Air

Does this sound anything like you? If you're a Libran, you're supposed to be affectionate and well-liked, fair-minded and easy-going. On the downside, you might also be accused of being indecisive and changeable.

September Birthdays

1 September
On 1 September 1985, a US-French expedition found the wreck of *RMS Titanic* at the bottom of the Atlantic Ocean. It sank in 1912 with a loss of around 1,500 lives.
You share a birthday with:
Edgar Rice Burroughs, writer (1875), Gloria Estefan, singer (1957).

2 September
On 2 September 1666, the Great Fire of London started. It raged for three days, destroying around 13,200 houses and making about one-sixth of the city's population homeless. And on 2 September 1945, Japan surrendered to the Allies, ending the Second World War.
You share a birthday with:
Keanu Reeves, actor (1964), Salma Hayek, actress (1968).

3 September
On 3 September 1935, a new land-speed record was set by Malcolm Campbell, who made an average speed of 301.129 mph on the salt flats of Utah, USA.
You share a birthday with:
Patriarch Peter VII of Alexandria (1949), Ferdinand Porsche, car designer (1875), Charlie Sheen, actor (1965).

4 September
On 4 September 476 AD, the Western Roman Empire came to an end when German Odoacer deposed Romulus Augustus, the last Emperor of Rome, and proclaimed himself King of Italy.
You share a birthday with:
King Alexander III of Scotland (1241), Joan Aiken, writer (1924), Beyoncé Knowles, singer (1981).

5 September
On 5 September 1977, Mother Teresa died in India. She was a nun who devoted her life to helping the poor and dying of Calcutta.
You share a birthday with:
Jesse James, US outlaw (1847), Raquel Welch, actress (1940), Freddie Mercury, singer with Queen (1946).

6 September
On 6 September 1522, Ferdinand Magellan's expedition completed the first circumnavigation of the world (although Magellan had been killed in the Philippines the previous year).
You share a birthday with:
Tsar Ivan VI of Russia (1666), Greg Rusedski, tennis player (1973), Tim Henman, tennis player (1974).

7 September
On 7 September 1838, lighthouse keeper's daughter, Grace Darling, saved the lives of nine people from the *SS Forfarshire*, which had run aground. She became a Victorian heroine.
You share a birthday with:
Elizabeth I of England (1533), Buddy Holly, singer (1936).

8 September
On 8 September 1664, New Amsterdam was renamed New York. And on 8 September 1966, *Star Trek* was first shown on television.
You share a birthday with:
Richard I of England (1157), Peter Sellers, actor and comedian (1925), Pink, singer (1979).

9 September
On 9 September 1976, Chinese revolutionary and statesman Chairman Mao died.
You share a birthday with:
Otis Redding, singer/songwriter (1941), Hugh Grant, actor (1960), Adam Sandler, actor and comedian (1966), Rachel Hunter, model (1969).

10 SEPTEMBER
On 10 September 1823, Simon Bolivar was made President of Peru. He fought for independence in Venezuela, Colombia, Ecuador, Peru, Panama and Bolivia, and is revered as a hero throughout much of Latin America. 10 September is also Gibraltar's national day.
You share a birthday with:
King Louis IV of France (920), Colin Firth, actor (1960), Guy Ritchie, film director and Mr Madonna (1968).

> **Canadian Birthdays**
> In some parts of Canada it's a tradition to grease someone's nose if it's their birthday.

11 SEPTEMBER
On 11 September 1297, the Scots, led by William Wallace, defeated the English at the Battle of Stirling Bridge. On 11 September 1962, the Beatles recorded their debut single, "Love Me Do".
You share a birthday with:
D H Lawrence, writer (1885), Moby, musician (1965), Harry Connick Jr, singer and actor (1967).

12 SEPTEMBER
On 12 September 1940, the Lascaux cave paintings, were discovered near Montignac, France.
You share a birthday with:
King Francis I of France (1494), Henry Hudson, explorer (1575), Jesse Owens, athlete (1913), Michael Ondaatje, writer (1943).

13 SEPTEMBER
On 13 September 122 AD work began on the construction of Hadrian's Wall.

You share a birthday with:
J B Priestley, writer (1894), Roald Dahl, writer (1916).

14 SEPTEMBER
On 14 September 1868, the first recorded "hole in one" was scored by Scottish golfer Tom Morris. On 14 September 1952, the Soviet *Lunar 2* became the first man-made object to reach the moon's surface.
You share a birthday with:
Michael Haydn, composer (1747), Sam Neill, actor (1947).

15 SEPTEMBER
On 15 September 1928, scientist Alexander Fleming discovered a mould that killed bacteria, which was later named penicillin.
You share a birthday with:
Agatha Christie, writer (1890), Tommy Lee Jones, actor (1946), Sophie Dahl, model (1979), Prince Harry of the United Kingdom (1984).

16 SEPTEMBER
On 16 September 1620, 102 pilgrims sailed on the *Mayflower* from Plymouth, England, to found a settlement in the New World (North America).
You share a birthday with:
Lauren Bacall, actress (1924), David Copperfield, magician (1956), Mickey Rourke, actor (1956), Katie Melua, singer (1984).

17 SEPTEMBER
On 17 September 1976, NASA unveiled the first space shuttle, the *Enterprise*.
You share a birthday with:
Frederick Ashton, ballet dancer and choreographer (1903), Anne Bancroft, actress (1931), Anastacia, singer (1973).

18 SEPTEMBER
On 18 September 96 AD, Nerva became Emperor of Rome. And 18 September is

also the feast day of Saint Joseph of Cupertino, a holy man who is believed to have been able to levitate.
You share a birthday with:
Samuel Johnson, writer (1709), Greta Garbo, actress (1905), Lance Armstrong, cyclist (1971), Jada Pinkett Smith, actress (1971).

19 SEPTEMBER

On 19 September 1893, all women in New Zealand were given the right to vote. On 19 September 1900, famous US outlaws Butch Cassidy and the Sundance Kid committed their first robbery. And on 19 September 1991, Otzi the ice man was discovered.
You share a birthday with:
King Henry III of France (1551), Zandra Rhodes, fashion designer (1940), Twiggy, model (1949), Victoria Silvstedt, model (1974).

20 SEPTEMBER

On 20 September 1967, the ocean liner the *Queen Elizabeth 2* was launched by Queen Elizabeth II at Clydebank, Scotland. The prestigious cruise liner is one of the fastest passenger ships afloat.
You share a birthday with:
Alexander the Great, general (356 BC), Sophia Loren, actress (1934).

21 SEPTEMBER

On 21 September 1792, the monarchy was abolished in France and the First Republic was established. On 21 September 1937, the novel *The Hobbit* by JRR Tolkien was published.
You share a birthday with:
H G Wells, writer (1866), Stephen King, writer (1947), Nicole Richie, socialite and celebrity (1981).

22 SEPTEMBER

On 22 September 2003, Englishman David Hempelman-Adams became the first person ever to cross the Atlantic Ocean in an open-basket hot-air balloon.
You share a birthday with:
Anne of Cleves, fourth wife of Henry VIII (1551), Michael Faraday, scientist (1791), Fay Weldon, writer (1931), Ronaldo, footballer (1976), Billie Piper, singer and actress (1982).

23 SEPTEMBER

On 23 September 490 BC, the Greeks defeated the Persians in the Battle of Marathon. Legend says that a Greek herald ran from the battlefield to Athens to announce the victory. This inspired the first modern marathon running race, held during the 1896 Olympics.
You share a birthday with:
Euripides, playwright (480 BC), King Ferdinand VI of Spain (1713), Bruce Springsteen, singer (1949).

> "Eeyore is in a Very Sad Condition, because it's his birthday, and nobody has taken any notice of it, and he's very Gloomy."
> — A A Milne, Winnie-the-Pooh

24 SEPTEMBER

24 September is the date of Barcelona's Fiesta de la Mercé.
You share a birthday with:
Vitellius, Roman Emperor (15 AD), Jim Henson, creator of *The Muppets* (1936), Linda McCartney, singer (1941), Lars Emil Johansen, former Prime Minister of Greenland (1946).

25 September

On 25 September 275 AD, Tacitus became Emperor of Rome. And on 25 September 1066, King Harold of England defeated a Viking army at the Battle of Stamford Bridge.
You share a birthday with:
Michael Douglas, actor (1944), Christopher Reeve, *Superman* actor (1952), Will Smith, singer and actor (1968), Catherine Zeta Jones, actress (1969), Jodie Kidd, model (1978).

26 September

On 26 September 1580, Francis Drake became the first British explorer to sail around the world. His ship was called the *Golden Hind*.
You share a birthday with:
T S Eliot, poet (1888), George Gershwin, composer (1898), Olivia Newton-John, singer and actress (1948), Serena Williams, tennis player (1981).

27 September

On 27 September 1821, Mexico became independent from Spain.
You share a birthday with:
Meat Loaf, singer (1947), King Louis XIII of France (1601), Irvine Welsh, author (1961), Avril Lavigne, singer (1984).

28 September

On 28 September 48 BC, Pompey the Great was assassinated on the orders of King Ptolemy of Egypt. And on 28 September 1066, William the Conqueror invaded England.
You share a birthday with:
Caravaggio, artist (1573), Brigitte Bardot, actress (1934), Naomi Watts, actress (1968), Gwyneth Paltrow, actress (1973).

29 September

On 29 September 1978, Pope John Paul I died only thirty-three days after he'd become Pope. And 29 September is also the Christian feast day of Michaelmas (the feast day of Saint Michael and All Angels).
You share a birthday with:
Pompey the Great, Roman general and politician (106 BC), Miguel de Cervantes, writer (1547), Elizabeth Gaskell, writer (1810), Horatio Nelson, admiral (1758).

30 September

The premiere of the opera *The Magic Flute* by Mozart was held on 30 September 1791 in Vienna. The premiere of the opera *Porgy and Bess* by Gershwin was held on 30 September 1935 in Massachusetts.
You share a birthday with:
Truman Capote, writer (1924), Martina Hingis, tennis player (1980), Monica Bellucci, actress (1968).

Morning Glory

October

October was originally the eighth month of the Roman calendar (counting from March), so it's named after the Latin word for "eight". The Saxons called October *Wyn Monath* because it was the month for making wine.

Birthstone: Opal
Flower: Marigold
Star Signs: Libra (see page 149) and . . .

Scorpio (the Scorpion)
Dates: 24 October – 23 November
Ruling Planet: Pluto
Element: Water

Does this sound anything like you? If you're born under the sign of Scorpio, you're supposed to be emotional and creative with a magnetic personality. But you might find that you're accused of being moody and unforgiving.

October Birthdays

1 OCTOBER

On 1 October 1949, revolutionary Mao Zedung officially proclaimed the existence of the People's Republic of China, with himself head of state.
You share a birthday with:
Henry III of England (1207), Frederick I of Denmark (1471), Jimmy Carter, former US President (1924), Julie Andrews, *Mary Poppins* and *The Sound of Music* actress (1935).

2 OCTOBER

On 2 October 1836, scientist Charles Darwin returned to England, aboard the *HMS Beagle*, after a five-year expedition to the southern Atlantic and Pacific Oceans, and went on to develop his theory of evolution.
You share a birthday with:
King Richard III of England (1452), Mahatma Gandhi, Indian leader (1869), Graham Greene, writer (1904), Sting, musician (1951).

3 OCTOBER

On 3 October 1906, the Berlin Radiotelegraphic Conference decided that SOS would become the international distress signal. Contrary to popular belief, the letters were chosen not because they stand for "Save Our Souls" but because they were easy to transmit in Morse Code.
You share a birthday with:
Leopold II, Grand Duke of Tuscany (1797), Gore Vidal, writer (1925), Gwen Stefani, singer (1969).

4 OCTOBER

On 4 October 1957, the Soviet Union launched *Sputnik*, the world's first artificial satellite.
You share a birthday with:
King Louis X of France (1289), King Charles IX of Sweden (1550), Susan Sarandon, actress (1946).

5 OCTOBER

On 5 October 1974, American David Kunst completed the first round-the-world journey on foot, which had taken him four years. And on 5 October 1989, the Dalai Lama, the exiled religious and political leader of Tibet, was awarded the Nobel Peace Prize.
You share a birthday with:
Sir Bob Geldof, musician and humanitarian (1954), Kate Winslet, actress (1975).

6 OCTOBER

On 6 October 1847, Charlotte Brontë's *Jane Eyre* was published, under the pseudonym Currer Bell.
You share a birthday with:
King Wenceslaus III of Bohemia (1289), King Louis-Philippe of France (1773), Britt Ekland, actress (1942).

7 OCTOBER

On 7 October 1949, East Germany was proclaimed a republic within the Soviet Union, with Wilhelm Pieck as the country's first president.
You share a birthday with:
King Charles XIII of Sweden (1748), Desmond Tutu, archbishop and anti-apartheid campaigner (1931), Yo-yo Ma, cellist (1955), Simon Cowell, record executive and TV personality (1959).

8 OCTOBER

On 8 October 1895, Queen Min of Joseon, the last empress of Korea, was assassinated. And on 8 October 1967, revolutionary Che Guevara and his men were captured in Bolivia. Next day, Guevara was executed by firing squad.
You share a birthday with:
Sigourney Weaver, actress (1949), Paul Hogan, actor (1939), Matt Damon, actor (1970).

October

9 October
On 9 October 1963, Uganda became a republic. And on 9 October 1940, St Paul's Cathedral in London was bombed during the Battle of Britain in the Second World War.
You share a birthday with:
King Dinis of Portugal (1261), King Charles X of France (1767), John Lennon, musician (1940), Sharon Osbourne, music manager and TV personality (1952).

10 October
On 10 October 1881, Charles Darwin published his book *The Formation of Vegetable Mould Through the Action of Worms*, which he considered to be his most important work. And on 10 October 1970, Fiji became an independent country.
You share a birthday with:
Queen Isabella II of Spain (1832), Harold Pinter, playwright (1930), Chris Tarrant, TV presenter (1946).

11 October
On 11 October 1689, Peter the Great became emperor of Russia. And on 11 October 1968, *Apollo 7*, the first manned Apollo mission, was launched.
You share a birthday with:
King Frederick IV of Denmark (1671), Eleanor Roosevelt, First Lady of the United States (1884), Dawn French, comedian and actress (1957).

12 October
On 12 October 1957, the Lovell telescope – the world's first giant radio telescope – went into operation at Jodrell Bank Experimental Station in Cheshire, England.
You share a birthday with:
Leopold II of Austria (1095), King Edward VI of England (1537), Luciano Pavarotti, opera singer (1935), Hugh Jackman, actor (1968).

13 October
On 13 October 54 AD, Roman Emperor Claudius I died – probably poisoned by his wife, Agrippina.
You share a birthday with:
Emperor Konin of Japan (709 AD), Margaret Thatcher, former UK Prime Minister (1925), Sacha Baron Cohen, "Ali G" comedian (1971), Ashanti, singer (1980).

14 October
On 14 October 1066, William the Conqueror defeated King Harold of England at the Battle of Hastings. And on 14 October 1947, US Air Force Captain Chuck Yeager became the first person to fly faster than the speed of sound.
You share a birthday with:
Roger Moore, actor, (1927), Ralph Lauren, fashion designer (1939).

15 October
On 15 October 1997, the world's first supersonic land-speed record was set by the ThrustSSC team – 1227 km/h. On 15 October 2003, China launched its first manned space mission, *Shenzhou 5*.
You share a birthday with:
Virgil, Roman poet (70 BC), P G Wodehouse, writer (1881), Sarah Ferguson, Duchess of York (1959).

16 October
On 16 October 1793, former Queen Marie-Antoinette of France was guillotined. On 16 October 1958, *Blue Peter*, the most popular children's TV programme ever, was broadcast for the first time.
You share a birthday with:
James II of Scotland (1430), Oscar Wilde, writer (1854), Tim Robbins, actor (1958).

17 October
On 17 October 1346, King David II of Scotland was captured by King Edward III of England and imprisoned in the Tower of London for eleven years.

You share a birthday with:
Rita Hayworth, actress (1918), Evel Knievel, motorcycle stuntman (1938), Eminem, rapper (1972), Wyclif Jean, singer (1972).

18 OCTOBER

On 18 October 1469, Ferdinand of Aragon married Isabella of Castile, uniting Aragon and Castile into one country, Spain.
You share a birthday with:
Pope Pius II (1405), Chuck Berry, singer (1926), Martina Navratilova, tennis player (1956), Jean-Claude Van Damme, martial arts expert and actor (1960).

> **Saint Luke's Day**
> Saint Luke's Day falls on 18 October. On this day, girls are supposed to be able to find out their marriage prospects, by smearing their faces with honey, spices and vinegar before bedtime and reciting a rhyme. They're then supposed to dream of their future husband!

19 OCTOBER

On 19 October 1453, the Hundred Years War between England and France ended.
You share a birthday with:
John Le Carré, writer (1931), Philip Pullman, writer (1946), Evander Holyfield, boxer (1962), Trey Parker, cartoonist and creator of *South Park* (1969).

20 OCTOBER

On 20 October 1714, George I became King of the United Kingdom. And on 20 October 1973, the Sydney Opera House opened for the first time.
You share a birthday with:
Christopher Wren, architect (1632), King Stanislaus I of Poland (1677), Viggo Mortensen, actor (1958), Snoop Dogg, rapper (1972).

21 OCTOBER

On 21 October 1805, Admiral Horatio Nelson died at the Battle of Trafalgar, having defeated the French and Spanish fleets.
You share a birthday with:
Hongwu, Emperor of China (1328), Samuel Taylor Coleridge, poet (1772), Dizzy Gillespie, jazz musician (1917), Carrie Fisher, actress (1956).

22 OCTOBER

On 22 October 1797, the first parachute jump was made by André-Jacques Garnerin, who leaped out of a hydrogen balloon above Paris.
You share a birthday with:
Doris Lessing, writer (1919), Jeff Goldblum, actor (1952), Shaggy, singer (1968).

23 OCTOBER

On 23 October 1642, the first battle of the English Civil War took place – the Battle of Edgehill.
You share a birthday with:
Pelé, Brazilian footballer (1940), Michael Crichton, writer (1942).

24 OCTOBER

On 24 October 1901, Annie Edson Taylor made the first wooden-barrel ride over the Niagara Falls, starting a stunt tradition.
You share a birthday with:
Domitian, Emperor of Rome (51 AD), Kevin Kline, actor (1948), Roman Abramovich, billionaire businessman (1966), Caprice Bourret, model (1971), Wayne Rooney, footballer (1985).

25 October

On 25 October 1415, Henry V led the English to victory over the French at the Battle of Agincourt.
You share a birthday with:
Pablo Picasso, artist (1881), Anne Tyler, writer (1941), Nancy Cartwright, "Bart Simpson" voice actress (1959).

26 October

On 26 October 1863, the Football Association was formed. On 26 October 1881, the Gunfight at the OK Corral took place in Tombstone, Arizona. And on 26 October 1905, Norway became independent from Sweden.
You share a birthday with:
Mohammad Reza Shah Pahlavi, Shah of Iran (1919), Bob Hoskins, actor (1942), Andrew Motion, poet (1952).

27 October

On 27 October 1904, the New York City subway opened – today, the system is the largest in the world.
You share a birthday with:
Theodore Roosevelt, US President (1858), Dylan Thomas, poet (1914), Sylvia Plath, poet (1932), John Cleese, actor and comedian (1939), Kelly Osbourne, singer (1984).

28 October

On 28 October 306 AD Maxentius became Emperor of Rome. And on 28 October 1886 US President Cleveland dedicated the Statue of Liberty in New York Harbour.
You share a birthday with:
Evelyn Waugh, writer (1903), Francis Bacon, artist (1909), Bill Gates, computer pioneer (1955), Julia Roberts, actress (1967.

29 October

On 29 October 1618, Sir Walter Raleigh, explorer, was beheaded for conspiracy against King James I.
You share a birthday with:
Henry III, Holy Roman Emperor (1017), Richard Dreyfuss, actor (1947), Yasmin Le Bon, model (1964), Winona Ryder, actress (1971).

30 October

On 30 October 1811, Jane Austen's *Sense and Sensibility* was published. And on 30 October 1938, Orson Welles broadcast a radio version of H G Wells' novel *The War of the Worlds* and caused panic across America as people believed they were being invaded by Martians.
You share a birthday with:
Ezra Pound, poet (1885), Diego Armando Maradona, football player (1960), Gavin Rossdale, singer (1967).

31 October

On 31 October 1892, *The Adventures of Sherlock Holmes* by Arthur Conan Doyle was published. And, of course, 31 October is Halloween.
You share a birthday with:
King Ferdinando I of Portugal (1345), Jan Vermeer, artist (1632), Pope Clement XIV (1705), John Keats, poet (1795), John Candy, actor and comedian (1950).

Marigold

November

November is the eleventh month of the year, but in the original Roman calendar it was the ninth month, and that's what the name means. For the Saxons it was the month of blood (when animals were slaughtered) and cold winds. The beginning of November has always been a time to celebrate the end of the harvest and the beginning of winter.

Birthstone: Topaz
Flower: Chrysanthemum
Star Signs: Scorpio (see page 155) and . . .

Sagittarius (the Archer)
Dates: 24 November – 23 December
Ruling Planet: Jupiter
Element: Fire

Does this sound anything like you? If you're a Sagittarian, you're supposed to be warm, optimistic, outgoing and adaptable. You might also be accused of being tactless, careless and boastful.

November Birthdays

1 NOVEMBER

On 1 November 1512, Michelangelo's artwork in the Sistine Chapel, Rome, was shown to the public for the first time.
You share a birthday with:
King Louis II ("the Stammerer") of West Francia (846 AD), Gustav IV Adolf of Sweden (1778), L S Lowry, artist (1887), Jenny McCarthy, TV presenter, model and actress (1972), Aishwarya Rai, Bollywood actress and model (1973).

2 NOVEMBER

On 2 November 1947, the *Spruce Goose*, the largest aircraft ever built, made its first and only flight. 2 November is also the Day of the Dead in Mexico, when families remember loved ones by decorating their graves and holding special meals in their memory.
You share a birthday with:
Marie Antoinette, Queen of France (1755), Burt Lancaster, actor (1913), k d lang, singer (1961), Nelly, singer (1974).

3 NOVEMBER

On 3 November 1928, Mickey Mouse made his debut appearance in *Steamboat Willie*. And on 3 November 1957, the Soviet Union launched the first animal into space – a dog called Laika – on the *Sputnik 2* spacecraft.
You share a birthday with:
King Edward V of England (1470), Osman II, Sultan of Turkey (1604), Charles Bronson, actor (1921), Lulu, singer (1948).

"We're fools whether we dance or not, so we might as well dance."
– Japanese proverb

4 November

On 4 November 1922, Howard Carter and his team discovered the entrance to the tomb of King Tutankhamen in the Valley of the Kings in Egypt.
You share a birthday with:
William of Orange, King of England (1650), Laura Bush, former US First Lady (1946), Puff Daddy, rapper (1969).

5 NOVEMBER

On 5 November 1605, King James I discovered a plot to blow up the Houses of Parliament. 5 November is Guy Fawkes Night, remembering one of the plotters.
You share a birthday with:
Ibrahim I, Ottoman Sultan (1615), Vivien Leigh, actress (1913), Sam Shepard, actor (1943), Bryan Adams, singer (1959).

6 NOVEMBER

On 6 November 1860, Abraham Lincoln became President of the United States.
You share a birthday with:
Joanna the Mad, Queen of Castille (1479), Suleiman the Great, Sultan of Turkey (1494), Thomas Kyd, playwright (1558), King Charles II of Spain (1661), Ethan Hawke, actor and film director, (1970).

7 NOVEMBER

On 7 November 1984, Ronald Reagan won a second term as US President. And on 7 November 1998, the world's oldest astronaut, seventy-seven-year-old John Glenn, landed safely back on Earth after a nine-day space mission.
You share a birthday with:
Marie Curie, scientist (1867), Leon Trotsky, Russian revolutionary (1879), Joni Mitchell, singer (1943), Rio Ferdinand, footballer (1978).

8 NOVEMBER

On 8 November 1793, the Louvre, a former royal palace, was opened as a public museum by the French revolutionary government. You share a birthday with: Nerva, Roman Emperor (35 AD), Bram Stoker, writer of *Dracula* (1847), Tara Reid, actress (1975), Jack Osbourne, TV personality (1985).

9 November
On 9 November 1960, John F Kennedy was voted in as the youngest ever US President.
You share a birthday with:
Katherine Hepburn, actress (1909), Nick Lachey, singer (1973), Sisqo, singer (1978).

10 November
On 10 November 1871, Henry Stanley found explorer David Livingstone, greeting him with the words "Dr Livingstone, I presume?" And on 10 November 1928, Hirohito became Emperor of Japan.
You share a birthday with:
Martin Luther, protestant reformer (1483), William Hogarth, artist (1697), Richard Burton, actor (1925), Brittany Murphy, actress (1977).

11 November
On 11 November 1918, at the eleventh hour of the eleventh day of the eleventh month, the First World War ended.
You share a birthday with:
Fyodor Dostoevsky, writer (1821), Demi Moore, actress (1962), Leonardo di Caprio, actor (1974).

12 November
On 12 November 1980, US spacecraft *Voyager 1* sent back photographs from Saturn, showing the planet's famous rings. And on 12 November 1990, Akihito became Emperor of Japan.
You share a birthday with:
Auguste Rodin, sculptor (1840), Grace Kelly, actress and Princess of Monaco (1929), David Schwimmer, actor (1966).

13 November
On 13 November 1971, the US space probe *Mariner 9* became the first spacecraft to orbit another planet as it went into orbit around Mars.
You share a birthday with:
King Edward III of England (1312), Jiaging, Emperor of China (1760), Robert Louis Stevenson, writer (1850), Whoopi Goldberg, actress and comedian (1955).

14 November
On 14 November 1851, *Moby Dick* by Herman Melville was published. And on 14 November 1969, *Apollo 12* was launched, the second manned mission to the moon.
You share a birthday with:
Claude Monet, artist (1840), Charles, Prince of Wales (1948).

15 November
On 15 November 1889, Pedro II of Brazil was deposed and the country became a republic. On 15 November 1968, BBC 1 and ITV began broadcasting in colour.
You share a birthday with:
Georgia O'Keefe, artist (1887), Richmal Crompton, *Just William* writer (1890), J G Ballard, writer (1930).

16 November
On 16 November 1384, Hedwig was crowned King of Poland, despite being a woman. And on 16 November 2001, the first Harry Potter film was released.
You share a birthday with:
Tiberius, Emperor of Rome (42 BC), David Kalakaua, King of Hawaii (1836), Paul Scholes, footballer (1974).

17 November
On 17 November 1558, Elizabeth I became Queen of England.

You share a birthday with:
King Louis XVIII of France (1785), Queen Astrid of Belgium (1905), Martin Scorsese, director (1942), Danny De Vito, actor (1944), Lisa Bonet, actress (1967).

> "The manner of giving is worth more than the gift."
> — Pierre Corneille

18 NOVEMBER

On 18 November 1991, Terry Waite, a hostage held in Beirut since 1987 during the Lebanese civil war, was freed and returned home to Britain.
You share a birthday with:
Vespasian, Roman Emperor (9 AD), Sojourner Truth, campaigner for the abolition of slavery and women's rights (1787), Margaret Atwood, writer (1939), Owen Wilson, actor (1968).

19 NOVEMBER

On 19 November 1969, the famous Brazilian footballer Pelé scored his thousandth professional goal.
You share a birthday with:
Emperor Go-Kashiwabara of Japan (1464), Calvin Klein, fashion designer (1942) Meg Ryan, actress (1961), Jodie Foster, actress and director (1962).

20 NOVEMBER

On 20 November 1947, Princess Elizabeth (later Queen Elizabeth I of England) married Philip Mountbatten, who became known as the Duke of Edinburgh.
You share a birthday with:
Edwin Hubble, astronomer (1889), Emilio Pucci, fashion designer (1914), Nadine Gordimer, writer (1923), Bo Derek, actress (1956).

21 NOVEMBER

On 21 November 1783, Frenchmen Jean-Francois Piletre de Rozier and Francois Laurent made the first hot-air balloon flight.
You share a birthday with:
Voltaire, philosopher (1694), Goldie Hawn, actress (1945), Björk, singer (1965).

22 NOVEMBER

On 22 November 1718, the infamous pirate Blackbeard was killed off the North Carolina coast. On 22 November 1963, John Fitzgerald Kennedy, the US President, was assassinated in Dallas, Texas.
You share a birthday with:
George Eliot, novelist (1819), Benjamin Britten, composer (1913), Boris Becker, tennis player (1967), Scarlett Johanssen, actress (1984).

23 NOVEMBER

On 23 November 1874, *Far from the Madding Crowd* by Thomas Hardy was published. And on 23 November 1963, the first episode of the BBC TV series *Dr Who* was screened, with William Hartnell as the Doctor.
You share a birthday with:
Otto I the Great, Holy Roman Emperor (912 AD), Billy the Kid, US outlaw (1859 or 1860), Zoe Ball, TV and radio presenter (1970).

24 NOVEMBER

On 24 November 1434, the River Thames froze over. On the same date in 1715, it froze over again – and a "frost fair" was held on the ice. On 24 November 1859, Charles Darwin's *On the Origin of Species by Means of Natural Selection* was published.
You share a birthday with:
Spinoza, philosopher (1632), King Charles XI of Sweden (1655), Zachary Taylor, former US President (1794), Toulouse-Lautrec, artist (1864), Scott Joplin, musician (1868), Billy Connolly, comedian (1942).

25 November

On 25 November 1952, *The Mousetrap*, a murder-mystery by Agatha Christie, opened at the Ambassadors Theatre in London. It was still running after 20,000 performances.
You share a birthday with:
Lope de Vega, Spanish poet and playwright (1562), Joe Di Maggio, baseball player (1914), Rock Hudson, actor (1925).

26 November

On 26 November 1922, archaeologists Howard Carter and Lord Carnarvon entered King Tutankhamen's tomb – they were the first people to enter the tomb in over 3,000 years. On 26 November 1983, an armed gang stole £26 million of gold bullion from a warehouse at Heathrow Airport – most of it was never recovered.
You share a birthday with:
Emperor Go-Daigo of Japan (1288), Charles Schultz, *Charlie Brown* cartoonist (1922), Tina Turner, singer (1939), Natasha Bedingfield, singer (1981).

27 November

On 27 November 511 AD, Clovis, King of the Franks, died, and his kingdom (which was in part of modern-day France) was distributed amongst his four sons.
You share a birthday with:
Bruce Lee, martial arts expert and actor (1940), Jimi Hendrix, musician (1942).

28 November

On 28 November 1990, Margaret Thatcher left Number 10 Downing Street after eleven years as Prime Minister of Great Britain.
You share a birthday with:
John Bunyan, writer (1628), William Blake, poet and artist (1757), Anna Nicole Smith, model (1967).

29 November

On 29 November 1929, American explorer Richard Byrd and his team made the first flight over the South Pole.
You share a birthday with:
Zhentong, Emperor of China (1427), Louisa May Alcott, writer of *Little Women* (1832), C S Lewis, writer of *The Chronicles of Narnia* (1898), Jacques Chirac, President of France (1932).

30 November

On 30 November 1966, Barbados became an independent country. And on 30 November 1974, "Lucy", the skeleton of a hominid more than three million years old, was discovered in Ethiopia. 30 November is also Saint Andrew's Day. Saint Andrew is the patron saint of Scotland.
You share a birthday with:
Jonathan Swift, writer of *Gulliver's Travels* (1667), Mark Twain, writer of *Huckleberry Finn* (1835), Winston Churchill, former UK Prime Minister (1874), Ridley Scott, film director (1937).

Chrysanthemum

December

December was named as the tenth month by the Romans – though of course it's the twelfth month now. Saxons called December the Yule, or winter month. In the northern hemisphere, there has always been a mid-winter celebration around the time that Christmas is celebrated – people need something to cheer themselves up.

Birthstone: Turquoise
Flower: Holly or poinsettia
Star Signs: Sagittarius (see page 161) and . . .

Capricorn (the Goat)
Dates: 22 December – 20 January
Ruling Planet: Saturn
Element: Earth

Does this sound anything like you? If you're born under the sign of Capricorn, you're supposed to be shy but funny, ambitious and determined. On the downside, you might also tend to be gloomy and cold towards other people.

December Birthdays

1 December
On 1 December 1955, Rosa Parks was jailed for refusing to give up her bus seat to a white man, in violation of racial segregation laws in Alabama, sparking a successful civil rights campaign.
You share a birthday with:
King Louis VI of France (1081), Woody Allen, actor and film director (1935), Bette Midler, actress (1945).

2 December
On 2 December 1804, Napoleon was crowned Emperor of France in Notre Dame Cathedral in Paris.
You share a birthday with:
Maria Callas, singer (1923), Gianni Versace, fashion designer (1946), Lucy Liu, actress (1968), Britney Spears, singer (1981).

3 December
On 3 December 1967, the first human heart transplant was carried out in Cape Town, South Africa.
You share a birthday with:
Joseph Conrad, writer of *Heart of Darkness* (1857), Ozzy Osbourne, singer (1948), Julianne Moore, actress (1960).

4 December
On 4 December 1872, the *Mary Celeste*, an American ship, was sighted in the Atlantic Ocean – the ship was at full sail and still had its stores and supplies, but not a single person was on board.
You share a birthday with:
Crazy Horse, Native American leader (1849), Wassily Kandinsky, painter (1866), Marisa Tomei, actress (1964).

5 December
On 5 December 1933, the national prohibition of alcohol in the US was ended.
You share a birthday with:
Pope Julius II (1443), Walt Disney, cartoon producer (1901), Frankie Muniz, *Malcolm in the Middle* actor (1985).

6 December
On 6 December 1921, the Irish Free State was declared. 6 December is also the feast day of Saint Nicholas, when children in Holland and France receive Christmas presents.
You share a birthday with:
King Ferdinand IV of Castile (1285), King Henry IV of England (1421), Nick Park, *Wallace and Gromit* film-maker (1958).

7 December
On 7 December 1941, the US fleet at Pearl Harbor was bombed by the Imperial Japanese Navy, drawing the United States into the Second World War.
You share a birthday with:
Marie Tussaud, waxwork modeller and museum owner (1761), Noam Chomsky, political writer (1928).

A Strange December Event
The men of Mamala and Morella villages in Bali beat each other with broomsticks in a strange event called Pakul Sapu that takes place every December. Then they apply a special coconut oil to their wounds.

8 DECEMBER

On 8 December 1980, John Lennon, former member of the Beatles, was assassinated in New York City. And on 8 December 1907, King Gustav V became King of Sweden.
You share a birthday with:
Horace, Roman poet (65 BC), Mary Queen of Scots (1542), Jim Morrison, singer (1943), Sinead O'Connor, singer (1966), Teri Hatcher, actress (1964).

9 DECEMBER

On 9 December 1931, Spain abolished its royal family and became a republic. And on 9 December 1960, *Coronation Street* was first shown on TV.
You share a birthday with:
John Milton, poet (1608), Judi Dench, actress (1934), John Malkovich, actor (1953).

10 DECEMBER

On 10 December 1901, the first Nobel Prizes were awarded in Stockholm, Sweden, in the fields of physics, chemistry, medicine, literature and peace.
You share a birthday with:
Ada Lovelace, computer programmer (1815), Emily Dickinson, poet (1830), Kenneth Branagh, actor and film director (1960).

11 DECEMBER

On 11 December 1946, the United Nations International Children's Emergency Fund (UNICEF) was founded.
You share a birthday with:
Pope Leo X (1485); Alexander Solzhenitsyn, Russian writer (1918), Sir Kenneth Macmillan, ballet dancer and choreographer (1929).

12 DECEMBER

On 12 December 1901, Guglielmo Marconi sent the first radio transmission across the Atlantic Ocean. And on 12 December 1913, the *Mona Lisa* was recovered in Florence, two years after it was stolen from the Louvre Museum in Paris.

You share a birthday with:
Gustave Flaubert, *Madame Bovary* writer (1821), Frank Sinatra, singer (1915).

13 DECEMBER

On 13 December 1577, Francis Drake set off from Plymouth – he returned three years later having made the first British circumnavigation of the earth. And on 13 December 1642, Abel Tasman became the first European to set foot in New Zealand.
You share a birthday with:
King Eric XIV of Sweden (1533), King Henry IV of France (1553), Dick Van Dyke, actor (1925), Jamie Foxx, actor (1967).

14 DECEMBER

On 14 December 1911, Norwegian explorer Roald Amundsen became the first person to reach the South Pole.
You share a birthday with:
Emperor Go-Suzaku of Japan (1009), Nostradamus, French astrologer and mathematician (1503), King George VI of the United Kingdom (1895), Michael Owen, footballer (1979).

15 DECEMBER

On 15 December 1791, the United States Bill of Rights, the first ten amendments of the American Constitution, was passed. The bill limited the federal government's powers, protecting the rights and freedom of the people. It plays a central role in American law to this day.
You share a birthday with:
Lucius Verus, Emperor of Rome (130 AD), Nero, Emperor of Rome (37 AD), J Paul Getty, billionaire oil magnate (1892), Adam Brody, actor (1979).

16 December

On 16 December 1653, Oliver Cromwell became Lord Protector of England, Scotland and Ireland. And on 16 December 1773, a group of Massachusetts colonists boarded three British ships in Boston harbour and dumped 342 chests of tea into the sea, in protest at trading laws – the event became famous as the Boston Tea Party.
You share a birthday with:
Catherine of Aragon, wife of Henry VIII (1485), Jane Austen, writer of *Pride and Prejudice* (1775), Noel Coward, playwright (1899), Benjamin Bratt, actor (1963).

17 December

On 17 December 1843, *A Christmas Carol* by Charles Dickens was published. And on 17 December 1903, Orville and Wilbur Wright made the first successful flight in a self-propelled, heavier-than-air aircraft.
You share a birthday with:
Emperor Go-Uda of Japan (1267), Ludwig van Beethoven (1770), Milla Jovovich, actress and model (1975).

18 December

On 18 December 1865, slavery was abolished in the United States.
You share a birthday with:
Steven Spielberg, film director (1946), Brad Pitt, actor (1964), Katie Holmes, actress (1978), Christina Aguilera, singer (1980).

19 December

On 19 December 1963, Zanzibar became independent from the United Kingdom. On 19 December 1972, *Apollo 17*, the last manned spaceflight to the moon, returned to Earth. And on 19 December 1997, the movie *Titanic* opened in cinemas (it went on to win eleven Oscars).
You share a birthday with:
King Philip V of Spain (1683), Edith Piaf, singer (1915), Alyssa Milano, actress (1972), Jake Gyllenhaal, actor (1980).

20 December

On 20 December 1803, the United States bought a huge chunk of land from France – more or less the whole middle section of the country – for $15 million.
You share a birthday with:
King John III of Sweden (1537), Uri Geller, psychic and spoon-bender (1946), Ashley Cole, footballer (1980).

21 December

On 21 December 1958, Charles de Gaulle was elected president of France. And on 21 December 1968, *Apollo 8*, the first manned spacecraft to reach the moon, was launched.
You share a birthday with:
Benjamin Disraeli, former UK Prime Minister (1804), Kiefer Sutherland, actor (1966).

> "I am thankful for the mess to clean after a party because it means I have been surrounded by friends."
> — Nancie J Carmody

22 December

On 22 December 1989, the Brandenburg Gate in Berlin opened for the first time in thirty years, ending the division between East and West Germany.
You share a birthday with:
Giacomo Puccini, composer (1858), Ralph Fiennes, actor (1962), Robin and Maurice Gibb, singers with the Bee Gees (1949).

23 December

On 23 December 1986, the aircraft *Voyager*

landed at Edwards Air Force Base in California, completing the first non-stop flight around the world.
You share a birthday with:
Emperor Akihito of Japan (1933), Queen Silvia of Sweden (1943), Jodie Marsh, model (1978).

24 DECEMBER
On 24 December 1777, Captain Cook was the first European to set foot on the island of Kiritimati, which he named Christmas Island. Ava Gardner, actress (1922), Jennifer Lopez, singer and actress (1970), Ricky Martin, singer (1971).

Holly Superstitions
On Christmas Eve, take three leaves of holly and write the initials of three of your admirers on them (no doubt you'll have trouble narrowing this down to just three). Put the leaves under your pillow and you will dream about the one you're going to marry. Alternatively, tie a piece of holly to each corner of your bed, then eat a roasted apple before you go to sleep. You'll find that your future husband will appear in your dreams.

25 DECEMBER
25 December is Christmas Day. On 25 December 1914, the Christmas truce of the First World War began, when the opposing sides played football, sang carols and exchanged gifts.
Sir Isaac Newton, scientist (1642), Humphrey Bogart, actor (1899), Dido, singer (1971).

26 DECEMBER
On 26 December 1606, Shakespeare's play *King Lear* was performed for the first time, at the court of King James I. And on 26 December 1898, Marie and Pierre Curie announced that they had discovered the radioactive element radium.
You share a birthday with:
Frederick II, Holy Roman Emperor (1194), Charles Babbage, mathematician and computer inventor (1791), Mao Tse-tung, Chinese military leader (1893), Jared Leto, actor (1971).

27 DECEMBER
On 27 December 1831, Charles Darwin set out from Plymouth, England, aboard the *HMS Beagle* on a five-year expedition across the Atlantic and Pacific oceans. And on 27 December 1904, *Peter Pan,* by James Barrie, opened in London .
You share a birthday with:
Louis Pasteur, scientist (1822), Gerard Depardieu, actor (1948).

28 DECEMBER
On 28 December 1065, Westminster Abbey was consecrated. And on 28 December 1981, the first American test-tube baby, Elizabeth Carr, was born.
You share a birthday with:
Maggie Smith, actress (1934), Denzel Washington, actor (1954), Nigel Kennedy, violinist (1956), Sienna Miller, actress and model (1981).

29 December

On 29 December 1170, Thomas Becket, Archbishop of Canterbury, was murdered on the steps of Canterbury Cathedral.
You share a birthday with:
Prince Gu of Korea (1931), Jude Law, actor (1972).

30 December

On 30 December 1922, the Union of Soviet Socialist Republics (USSR) was established, the first country in the world to be based on socialism.
You share a birthday with:
Titus, Emperor of Rome (AD 39), Rudyard Kipling, writer of *The Jungle Book* (1865), Tiger Woods, golfer (1975).

31 December

On 31 December 1879, American inventor Thomas Alva Edison gave the first public demonstration of his incandescent lightbulb.
You share a birthday with:
Pope Callixtus III (1378), Henri Matisse, artist (1869), Anthony Hopkins, actor (1937), Val Kilmer, actor (1959).

Daily Destinies

Do you know which day of the week you were born on? There's an old rhyme that makes predictions for each one.

Monday's child is fair of face,
Tuesday's child is full of grace,
Wednesday's child is full of woe,
Thursday's child has far to go,
Friday's child is loving and giving,
Saturday's child works hard for a living.
But the child that is born on the Sabbath day is fair and wise and good and gay.

Holly

Index

A
April 119-123
August 143-147

B
Birthday Cakes
    Recipes 86-93
    Decoration 93-97

C
Cards 81-85
Clothes 9, 15, 17, 19, 20, 21, 22, 23, 30-31

D
December 167-172
Decorations 10, 15-16, 17-18, 20, 21, 24, 26-30
Drinks 11, 36-40

F
February 107-111

Food
Party Food 31-36
Sleepover Food 56-57

G
Games 40-45, 57-60
Gifts 71-80
Guest List 9, 11

I
Icing 93-96
Invitations 12-14, 15, 17, 19,

J
January 101-105
June 131-135
July 137-141

M
March 113-117
Music 9, 10, 19,

Index

N
November 161-165

O
October 155-159

P
Parties 8-47
- Planning 9-14
- Rules 10-11
- Themes 14-25

Presents 71-80

S
September 149-153

Sleepovers 55-61
- Essentials 60
- Pyjama food 56-57
- Silly games 57-60
- Souvenirs 60-61

Star signs
- Aquarius 101
- Aries 113
- Cancer 131
- Capricorn 167
- Gemini 125
- Leo 137
- Libra 149
- Pisces 107
- Sagittarius 161
- Scorpio 155
- Taurus 119
- Virgo 143

Surprises 61-69

T
Treats 49-54

W
Wrapping 79-80

www.piccadillypress.co.uk

☆ The latest news on forthcoming books

☆ Chapter previews

☆ Author biographies

☆ Fun quizzes

☆ Reader reviews

☆ Competitions and fab prizes

☆ Book features and cool downloads

☆ And much, much more . . .

Log on and check it out!

Piccadilly Press